MY FOREVER BEST FRIEND

THE HIGHS, LOWS AND BREATHLESS
ADVENTURES OF A LIFE LIVED WELL WITH
TYPE 1 DIABETES

MY FOREVER BEST FRIEND

THE HIGHS, LOWS AND BREATHLESS
ADVENTURES OF A LIFE LIVED WELL
WITH TYPE 1 DIABETES

YVONNE WARNER

Thanks must go to my nephew Mickey who helped me design the book cover, showing Yvonne as a child, contemplating her newly-discovered shadow self, Type 1 Diabetes. She had no idea of what the future would hold, but she unconsciously embraced and chose it as her lifelong best friend

CONTENTS

MY FOREVER BEST FRIEND

I have a secret best friend.

My forever best friend has been with me almost all my life and, as with all best friends, we have seen the best and worst of each other over the years.

I look after my best friend and my best friend looks after me. We have a secret communication where she signals me when I'm in danger, and I make sure I'm always listening so I can react fast. If I do, she keeps me safe

We sometimes get the balance wrong and fall out. It happens. If I'm distracted and not paying attention to her needs, she can be resentful and snappy. Sometimes we've been to the edge and looked over the precipice. But you work at it and fix it, pull back from the danger zone, hug and make up, and you both get on with living life to the full, looking after each other.

I've learnt to respect and support my best friend at all times. The rewards for both of us are a shared and well-lived life, full of adventures.

This kind of relationship, where you are so close you are virtually two halves of the same person, is a long-term investment. Especially if your life depends on it.

You are about to read the story of how, as a little girl aged nine, I met my best friend, how we fought at first, until we learned to find a balance. And you're going to explore with me our shared, lifelong adventures together.

My forever, inseparable, best friend is Type 1 Diabetes. This is the story of how we learned to live together. And to love each other. Because without my best friend, I wouldn't be me. And I wouldn't, I think, have lived the exciting, adventurous life I've led. Or that we've led.

So, buckle up …

… and enjoy the ride.

Because I certainly have so far.

And I don't intend to stop anytime soon.

Yvonne Warner

"Life is either a daring adventure or it is nothing at all." – Helen Keller

PRELUDE: THE SECRET LIFE

Nobody knows

I found this note that I scribbled in my diary.
Every time you get in a car to drive, you do your bloods.
Every time you walk, run, do Pilates, swim, circuit train, you do your bloods - before, after and sometimes in the middle.

Every time you present a lecture, be a key note speaker, key participant in a meeting, sit on a negotiating body, attend your kids' performances, you do your bloods.

Every time you go out with friends, and family for a celebration, you do your bloods.

Theatre, Cinema, Concerts, Gigs, Opera? You do your bloods.

Why? Because you want to be normal, you don't want to draw attention to yourself or your loved ones, you want to be yourself. And the only way you can do that is to get your bloods right!

I haven't always got it right through the last fifty years, as you can see from some of the experiences recounted in these pages. But my family and friends have always been there for me. I love and thank them with all my heart.

DEDICATION

If you face extreme adversity and challenge with good humour, determination, and a refusal to be bowed by it, a strange thing happens.

You can find yourself surrounded by people who rally to your cause. Your extraordinary challenge - and how you respond to it - can inspire others to be their best for you, to raise their game, just as it can bring out the best in you.

This is one of the odd ways in which a lifelong challenge, one that you might feel sets you apart or holds you back, can in fact be a spur to living an extraordinary life, bringing people to you as a loving and powerful support network that helps lift you up, to achieve what you want to achieve, to live the life you want to live.

I have been blessed by such a network of people.

In order of when they appeared in my life (or I did in theirs), the people I want to dedicate this book to, without whom I could not have lived the daring adventure are:

My amazing Mum, Dad and Brother Graham.

My other wonderful immediate family and friends who saw me through childhood and then university.

My incredible Husband Tony.

My awesome work colleagues, extended family and circle of friends outside work.

My wonderful children and grandchild.

The dedicated professionals, in particular, my consultants, the specialist nurses, opticians, podiatrists, and Pharmacists and not to mention all the wonderful support staff, including my longstanding hairstylist, who have helped me manage and be a support to me over the years.

Mum & Dad

Big Bro and I

The family on location

Some members of my fantastic Hospital Diabetes Team

Bro, Sis-in-law, Hubby and I

Otis & Nanny Beep

Tony's brother Peter, Thomas and my nephew Tim

Otis & Nanny's first Christmas together

CHAPTER 1

WHEN LIFE WAS 'NORMAL'

T**he tracks of my years**

For each section of this book, I'll start by giving you a soundtrack of those years. Like a multimedia experience, if you will. If you really want to immerse yourself in the era I'm describing in these pages, put some of these on in the background as you read. Hearing them takes me straight back in time. Music is like a time machine. So, here's your time machine settings for the first ten years of my life.

The earliest tracks baby Yvonne – the heroine of our story - was exposed to, the soundtrack of her first few years, imbibed with her mother's milk, you might say, included Hello Dolly by Louis Armstrong and Sweet Lorraine by Nat King Cole.

These songs are forever linked to me and mine: Dolly was my grandmother's name, Doris (or Dot) my mum's, and my middle name is Lorraine, because Mum loved that Nat King Cole song so much.

If I was gifted a middle name to connect me with Mum's musical affection, I inherited an unlikely love affair with the saxophone from my dad's listening habits: he filled the house with saxophonist Max Gregor. I know we've still got that album somewhere. Dean Martin and Frank Sinatra were to be found crooning in the background when we got home from school, keeping Mum company as she cooked our tea.

But Mum didn't just stick with the golden oldies. She had an ear for the newer sounds, too. Tom Jones began joining us as our soundtrack growing up and, even more radically, Mum loved the Beach Boys and the Monkees, the wacky American band we enjoyed watching on TV (when we got one).

My brother Graham found his musical interests later in the 60's. This was the first hint of discord within the family listening ranks, a generational schism that you have to have at some point don't you: Mum and Dad were not impressed by the Rolling Stones or Led Zeppelin (whom I also loved) and the heavy rock bands Graham brought into the house in the tail end of the decade.

So, you have the soundtrack to these years. Time for the subject of our story to emerge. Here she comes …

A Black Country Girl

Once upon a time - 13 November 1961, to be precise - I was born in a small house in Lower Gornal, Dudley, West Midlands. For those who don't know, this sacred part of the world – which sits within the West Midlands of England - is known as the Black Country.

In the 19th century, Dudley and surrounding towns housed the steel forges of the industrial revolution, while local coalmining provided the power; the smoke and grime from both activities dusting the land and earning the area around this cluster of industrial towns its nickname.

It was a home birth, delivered by an exceptionally large midwife, described by my father, who was not scared of anyone, as formidable and "not to be messed with". Wisely, he stayed out of the way and left the hard work to the women.

If you've seen the BBC series Call The Midwife, you'll be able to picture the early sixties' semi : the style of the décor, the furniture and the clothes – can you see it in your mind's eye? - as Yvonne was ushered into this cradle of the Industrial Revolution, where her family roots sank as deep as the coal beneath their feet, by a midwife who hailed from a more recent period in Britain's history, as nurses and midwives from the

West Indies answered the country's call for help with the post-World War Two baby boom.

Now, there we are, with baby Yvonne wrapped and content in the loving arms of her mum, cosy in bed, the midwife fussing around, cleaning up, her job done, letting Dad in to this inner sanctum of women; Dad nodding his thanks courteously and carefully skirting the 'not to be messed with' large presence of the midwife, parking himself next to the bed to greet the new born and kiss his wife.

It's a moment of wonder and relief, isn't it, the first holding of a new baby safely delivered, especially in those days when 'safely delivered' wasn't to be taken for granted. So, picture the magical family scene for a moment, as if you're peering in through the bedroom window, back in 1961.

Now, as you dwell on this, the first scene in baby Yvonne's life, you need to know what this little bundle of life contained, within her DNA, what it meant to be born a Black Country Girl into this particular family.

A blend of Black Country military service, industrial and business heritage flowed through this little baby's veins. They didn't know it yet, but a steeliness of purpose (fittingly, given Dad's steel industry background, of which more shortly), went deep in those tiny bones, along with a sense of responsibility, hard work, self-reliance, independence, duty, love of family … more than you think could possibly fit into a tiny new-born. It was all there. Because we are where and who we come from, aren't we.

But we are also inviolably ourselves. And little Yvonne would turn out to be her own girl, and later her own woman, with a strong sense of fun, a love of music, and enjoyment of life inherited from her parents, plus a determination to form her own point of view, as well as all the Black Country girl qualities just mentioned.

As she would often say in later life, "Yo can tek the gal out of Gornal, but yo cor tek Gornal out of the gal." She is still, in fact, to be found there at least one day a week, 62 years later, looking after her step-mum and Buster the dog.

So, what of her immediate parents, the mum and dad peering down at her in our little new-born tableau above:

When Dad had been called up, he had served in the Royal Electrical and Mechanical Engineers (REME) in, among other places, the Suez Canal. When demobbed and back in civilian life, he went from there into forging. No, not that kind of forging. No dodgy money presses hiding in the basement. Drop forging of steel, which is the industry specialism the Black Country excelled in.

As an aside, the military background would seep down into Yvonne's future generations (her first grandchild has just been born and may be reading this one day). That grandchild's uncle Richard has just passed out from Sandhurst Military Academy. Also, Yvonne's husband to be (if we leap ahead a few chapters and decades, just for a momentary glimpse of where we are heading) had a father who worked for Monty (General Montgomery, a charismatic figure who helped us win the war, for those too young to know or remember). We've still got the telexes. (Like old texts, but on paper, sent by phoneline, printed and delivered in an envelope by the postie). He was granted a British Empire Medal after the fighting was over.

Just as steeped in wartime and post-wartime history and reinforcing the resilience and compassion that already ran down the Black Country side of the family was Tony's (little Yvonne's future beau and then husband – her Mr Darcy, if you're feeling romantic) mum, who helped repatriate people from the horrors of Auschwitz. You'll have to look it up – Google it - if you don't know about that, but make sure you have a hankie or box of tissues with you as that was one of those times in which unbelievable evil was meted out on one set of people by another set of people, so I'm going to brush past it here, as it's too painful and sad to go into in any detail other than to say it was Tony's mum that helped those who had survived it rebuild a life afterwards. There is always a way forward after a personal tragedy, as our little Yvonne was to find out for herself, in a few short years.

But we are getting ahead of ourselves. Back to Dad and Mum.

Baby Yvonne was dead lucky to be born into that family: Mum was lovely, very quiet, a real lady. Dad was strong, hard and determined They were opposite, basically, each with qualities she would learn from and absorb.

Like most Black Country people, both families had come from a background of poverty and worked their way up. My maternal grandmother had a chain shop (a shed, basically) in the back garden. Grandfather on that side of the family had lost a leg down the pit or possibly in the war. Both had died before little Yvonne made her appearance in the world, so the exact detail of where the leg was lost – locally, under the earth of the Black Country or in some corner of a foreign field - is lost in the mists of time. My maternal grandmother died with undiagnosed type 2 diabetes, the knowledge of which would be a contributing factor in why Mum, so happy cradling the newborn in our tableau here, was so distraught on hearing of her childhood diagnosis a few short years later.

Dad's family were from Netherton, and were a very hard, even domineering family. That imposing side to their nature can be seen in the way they left their mark on the area: Grandpa Stafford had a street named after him in Dudley and the family had a monument in the graveyard where Duncan Edwards, the legendary footballer, is buried. They ended up with houses they rented out and sweet shops. Great Grandfather on this side of the family was a tyrant, by all accounts: he kept a whip at his side at the dining table; woe betide anyone who spoke during the meal. Great Grandmother was apparently lovely and in the very latter years did eventually move out. Grandad used to go and wet shave Great Grandad every week. When Grandad said, during one of these shaving sessions, that he had a new grandson - my brother Graham – there was the first and possibly only sign that the hard man of the family had softened with age; Great Grandfather Stafford gave him a half-crown for Graham. He had never done such a thing before for anyone!

A lot of family stories have passed down about what life was like. Remember that Monty Python sketch where a group of northern men are exaggerating the poverty they grew up in, trying to outdo each other? "You were lucky, I was born in a puddle" – that kind of thing? Like all humour, there's a grain of truth in there, which is why people laugh in recognition at it. The wartime and post-war generation did come from poverty that it's hard to imagine now.

Dad, when he was young, for example, used to have to put cardboard in the soles of his shoes when they leaked because the family couldn't afford new ones. When my parents got their first house, when my brother was born, Dad cycled home from work down the main road from Dudley on his bike, with a roll of carpet under his arm, to make the house cosier for the new arrival, because he hadn't got a car.

He would work his way up to become Managing Director of the drop forging company he worked for and go all over the world. But we never forgot our roots. And I am still proud of them.

So, Dad forged his career in the hard world of tough men and steel. Peaky Blinders' watchers can picture those scenes of Tommy striding down the cobbled streets with the arc of sparks and flames emerging from the open doorway of the steelworks as he passed, to help you picture the kind of workplace we're talking about. A bit romanticised, but that depiction of industrial steelworks cheek by jowl with where people lived gives you a sense of the Dudley steelworks where Dad worked, as Birmingham, where that programme is set, is just up the road. The underlying danger of violence among these hard men of the steel was also there and Dad had to be hard himself to keep them in check. One Saturday morning, for example (Dad often went into work on a Saturday morning) he found himself confronted by two men in the Drop Forge. They were skinheads, just to help you picture it. They had been demanding an increase in wages for a while and he had refused. That morning they had decided to confront him, when no one else was around, to scare him into giving in. They clearly didn't know my dad well enough. The story goes he picked up a piece of 3 x 2 and said, "Come on then". They didn't, thankfully, and were dismissed the following week.

Dad was what you might politely call 'firm but fair' at work. He was seen as such a taskmaster, in fact, insisting that his people work hard and get it right, that his nickname among some of them was, less politely, Hitler, would you believe! A no-nonsense boss often got labelled like that in those days. But they respected him, because when things weren't going right with the forging he'd roll his shirtsleeves up, leave the office, get down onto the shop floor and work the drop hammer himself to sort it out. Little Yvonne and her big brother Graham were to see this for themselves when they worked with their dad in the school holidays years ahead.

Where Dad spent his workdays in a hard environment, that – for the purposes of our book here – you could say reflected the tough, disciplinarian (but loving) man that he was, Mum, by a happy contrast as we come to describe her now, was as soft and sweet as the completely different environment from Dad's that she worked in.

For Mum (before Graham and I came along) worked in the Willy Wonka-like paradise (as imagined by kids, that is) of the Cadbury chocolate factory. The Cadbury family were Midlands' Quakers. In searching for a form of industry that suited their religious values of not wanting to make anything that could be used for war (The Quakers are pacifists) – they had established The Midlands from the nineteenth century, in among its existing background of hard industry, coal, steel and man's toil, as the unlikely centre of the world's emerging chocolate and confectionery production. A soft centre in the heart of industrial Britain.

Now, it may sound fanciful, but if you picture for an instant a future Yvonne heading into work as a Director in the NHS with a steel girder under one arm and a box of Milk Tray under the other, you get a snapshot glimpse of how the work backgrounds and personalities of her parents might have influenced her. No- nonsense determination to make sure the right things were done efficiently and effectively under one arm balanced with empathy and compassion that led her to stand up for those who were marginalised or discriminated against and needed championing, perhaps, under the other. That's a theme we'll expand on when, later in our story, baby Yvonne goes into the world of work, but I just wanted to plant that image in your head as a seed for you to remember.

Mum – before becoming a mum - worked at Cadbury's in Bournville, Birmingham. She caught the coach from Netherton about seven o'clock every morning and they brought her and the other workers home at night. Her job was to ice the designs on the chocolates. They were fantastic employers – Bournville was famously designed as a model workplace where the workers were taken care of. Everybody wanted to work at Cadbury's. They had a fantastic social network. A couple of times when the weather was really bad and they couldn't get home, they'd head for the huge social club, where they had pull-down beds for them to use. They really looked after them. In those days they presented the ladies who got married - and they had thousands of employees - with a beautiful leather-bound Bible. They did so to Mum when she married Dad. That Bible was going to mean a lot to me in later years, as we will see in a future chapter.

The caring Cadbury's model of employment, and working for Dad in the holidays, which Yvonne did when she was older, observing his managerial style in action, combined to influence baby Yvonne's career direction and her management methods and style in later life, as we shall see. As did the cataclysmic event that is coming in the next chapter. But you'll have to wait with bated breath for that, as I need to turn your attention, dear reader, to someone else first - the other member of the immediate family. You met him in passing when his name was mentioned above; the fourth occupant of the family house in Gornal, who had got there three years before me and was probably peering into the room where I was born, his three-and-a-half-year old self wondering what all the fuss was about and probably why he had a sister instead of a little brother to play with. How was he going to play for Wolves when he grew up if he didn't have a little brother to kick the ball around with first?

My incredible big brother Graham – he teased me like all big brother's do when I was little, so I'm paying him back by leaving him hanging around in the wings until now to let him into the story – was born in 1958. Unlike me, he didn't come into the world at home, but up the road, in the old Rosemary Ednam Maternity Ward, Burton Road Hospital. The 7th of April 1958 was the exact day. It was an old workhouse and asylum, in fact, which I should tease him about here, but I'll let that one go.

On the day and time he emerged, by a strange quirk, they had no baby baskets available, so they brought him out for his parents to view, from the baby ward, on ….. (drum roll please)

… a silver platter! I kid you not. Now, the way I saw us as we grew up is that Graham was the one who could do no wrong, whereas I was the stubborn one who had to go her own way and that often earned me some parental disapproval. I always said that the silver platter must have come with an accompanying silver spoon as a symbol of our roles in the family: he'd got the silver spoon of privilege in his mouth because he was always cast as the good boy who could do no wrong and I was always cast as the bad girl, the black sheep.

In later years, I became familiar with where Graham made his entrance on a bed of silver, because I was hospitalised there at 14, with a blood sugar problem (all will be explained on that front in the next chapter) and, in the sixth form, with some other friends, worked there as a cleaner to earn some money, crossing picket lines to do so. Like I said, hard work was one of the values we were born into.

I need to jump out of the timeline still further here to tell you a funny little story about the black sheep thing. As I'm writing this, a jumper of Princess Diana's recently came up for sale and sold for thousands at auction. It was the jumper she famously wore once, the picture ending up in all the papers, with a flock of white sheep and one black sheep in the middle, which is how she apparently felt – an outsider in the Royal Family.

Now, I'm not saying I felt an outsider in mine – I was surrounded by love – but when we were a lot older, Graham bought me that exact same jumper as a Christmas present. It was an in-joke about the way I used to say I was the black sheep and he was always the good one. When Diana's went for thousands, he called me up to ask if I still had it. Gone in the mists of time, I said. I mean, it was decades old and you can't hang onto everything. He thought it might be worth a few bob or at least be a talking point – my Princess Diana jumper – if I still had it. I mention it here because it's a theme that will come up again in our story – little baby Yvonne growing into a rebel non-conformist who makes her own decisions and is determined to go her own way.

So, we have our initial cast of main characters. Surrounded, we mustn't forget, by a supporting cast of wonderful family (Aunts and Uncles) and neighbours - the kind of neighbourhood network of friends and connections that sustained us as our local community. The family itself wasn't one of those big, extended family: I only had two cousins, John and Paul. John tragically drowned in the canal at Horsely Heath when very young. Dad's sister, my Aunty Iris, had also died in her late teens from a heart condition.

I survived (a dramatic word, you might think, but the next chapter explains it) and I owe it to their upbringing and the absolute love and support of my family and friends, not least the absolute love and support of my big brother who watched my back (and I watched his). On that last point, there was the occasional lapse in my big brother extending his protective arm and wrapping it around little Yvonne to keep her safe. I always wanted to be one of the boys, so tried to muscle in on him and his friends; they were having none of it. Mrs H., a neighbour, went running in to my Mum one sunny lunchtime in the summer holidays to say the boys had sent me on a 3- wheeler bike down Brickiln lane, tied and blindfolded to it, for a dare. I had said I was game and the boys just watched me go; it was the neighbours who stepped in and saved me from careering into the main road, off which the Crooked House used to stand (more on that in a minute)! I also remember one night the lads were all having a peashooter fight and I volunteered to crawl under Dad's car to pick up the peas. Dad came out and was going to reverse off the drive with me still under there until they stopped him. I got a good hiding for that one and so did Graham.

So, I was raised there in Lower Gornal, Dudley, and survived it, apart from the occasional apparent efforts of Graham and his mates to scupper my chances. My childhood was brilliant, playing in the streets, fields and woods behind my home. We had holidays in Devon, we had hard times, but my parents never let us see that.

I loved drawing and making things. I built fairy houses in the garden, camps in the fields behind the house. I'll never forget there was work being done in the fields behind, and we ran off with planks and some of the other building material we found there and used them to build a play camp. When it rained, the builders loved it, because they just came and stopped with us in the camp, nice and dry, while they had their sandwiches for lunch.

I remember using an egg box to make a tiny wheelbarrow. I put a little jar in it with pansies out of the garden and gave it to our neighbour next door. She said she loved it and I remember that felt so good. She probably binned it, but it was my initiation into my love of floristry and design, which has recently returned to my life. Thank you, Mrs H.

We'd go out in the school holidays, first thing in the morning, adventuring, come back for lunch, go back out, then come back for tea. The freedom children had in those days to explore and be free and play was brilliant. That was our growing up. Until I was nine. When everything changed. Forgive me for lingering in this chapter for a while longer before we get to that one. I'm enjoying revisiting the idyllic childhood that came before.

The Gornal I grew up in burst onto the front pages of the national newspapers recently, as I write this, for unfortunate reasons. We lived up the road from the Crooked House pub –an ancient building that was claimed to be the 'wonkiest' pub in the country until, in September 2023, it was bought and mysteriously went up in flames in the middle of the night.

A couple of people were arrested on suspicion of arson, so the mystery may have been solved by the time you read this. When I drove past it the other day – my step-mum still lives in my late dad's bungalow and we have to pass it to get to her – local people had banners up calling for action, including one pleading "Rebuild it wonky!" and another saying "Noddy Holder, please help us!" For those who don't know – if so, shame on you! – Noddy Holder is a local hero, lead singer and songwriter with the pop group Slade, whom we as kids growing up in Gornal ended up watching on Top of The Pops, or in our latter years seeing them in concert at The Civic, Wolverhampton. Anyway, back to childhood Yvonne and the timeline of our story. We used to go to the bluebell woods every year. They were just behind the Crooked House. That was my treat with my mum. There were two big marl clay holes there from where the clay had been dug out for industry. They became unofficial open air swimming holes for the kids. I never went in them, but my brother did. When it was sunny and beautiful, you really wanted to go in the water. But I was still the good girl then, not yet the black sheep, so I didn't but I did swim in Himley Hall lake with my school pals in later years, which was where Graham and my dad taught me to fish. Just as well I stayed away from swimming in the marl clay holes, as it turned out: the little boy who lived opposite us went into that cold water one summer and didn't come out alive. He drowned, poor lad. Not surprisingly, they've filled them in now. Danger can lurk, ready to snatch away the wonders of childhood, as I was to find out in a few short years myself.

I went to Redhall primary school in Gornal, which is still there. I loved art and making things at school. When I got home, I used to sit in my bedroom, pretending to be a teacher, reading to the children, making up my own stories, making friezes and pinning them to my wall. I'd have to do it without Dad knowing – he'd go ape at the holes in the wall - so I'd roll them up and put them in the wardrobe before he got home from work, making sure the drawing pin holes were covered by the curtains.

I've always loved interior design. I got top marks in school for anything art or craft-based. I just loved it. If I had my time again, I think I'd have gone into interior design because I love it so. Of course, I loved working in health, but when I retired, I went back to that fork in the road from all those decades ago and wove art and design back into my life. I was a Trustee for The Friends of Birmingham and museum Art Gallery. I also did my City and Guilds in Creative Floral Design (the seeds of Mrs H's praise for my pansies in an eggbox bearing very late fruit decades later) and I am now working with my nephew on photographic wall art images, all expressions of interest gratefully received.

OK, I've put it off long enough, indulging you (and myself) with these memories of an idyllic childhood. Before the big change happened. I've purposely lingered here, because this life of freedom, roaming and playing outside, was cut short by events in the next chapter, after which my sense of independence and adventure was curtailed. I could no longer go where I wanted, when I wanted. So, I'll finish off this chapter by sharing with you the happiest time of my day at school before my life changed – the last half hour. (No, not because it meant the school day was almost over!)

My fondest school memories involve the last 30 minutes of the school day, sat in front of a real open fire with Miss Winnie, who terrified us, except for that time at the close of the school day, where she brought our imaginations alive, reading us a story. My favourites were Enid Blyton's Famous Five stories. God bless Miss Winnie, because she got me into reading. Thanks to that, from a very young age I have always wanted to write a book. So, these pages you are reading are a direct consequence of Miss Winnie's influence and those afternoons drowsing in front of the fire and being transported through the stories she read us. It, like the rest of my young childhood in memory, was a magical time. My daughter, who is a schoolteacher, says Health & Safety rules today would have people throwing up their hands in horror at all those kids in front of an open fire. I've chosen that warm, favourite memory to end this chapter, because that provides a symbolic cosy end to that idyllic period of little Yvonne's life, as her plans for the future were beginning to be played out in her room at home – like the last thirty minutes of bliss at the end of the school day - before something scary came along to turn her idyllic childhood upside down.

You can stop holding your breath now. It's coming in the next chapter.

My Dad in the REME

Nanny Irene

My Mum and I

CHAPTER 2

EVERYTHING CHANGES

The tracks of my years

What a year for music in our house this was! My mum and dad had bought their first radiogram, a Grundig, in 1969. For any younger generation readers, that means you could play records on it as well as listen to the radio. Vinyl records. Graham and I headed to Stantons in Dudley, to buy our first singles or '45s' as they were called (because they revolved 45 times a minute, would you believe). Graham, as the older had first choice, and went for Sugar Sugar by the Archies, (which I wanted. Grrr).

It was Number 1 in the Charts and everybody loved it. He was the oldest, so had first choice. I've never forgiven him. As consolation, I chose Tracey by The Cufflinks. But Graham did let me play his 45 anytime I wanted. We played them endlessly. Stantons became a regular Saturday trip and we'd amassed a few records by 1971, which is where our story takes a turn. If you've found those two tracks on Spotify or wherever you find your music, and are listening along as you read, to help immerse yourself with travelling back into the past, it's lucky that they're easy listening and upbeat. Because you might need a cheering backdrop to the opening of this chapter …

* * *

There was something wrong with little Yvonne.

It had begun about halfway through her eighth year: She was often listless; her perennial sparkle had dimmed; she didn't seem to be the boisterous, enthusiastic little girl she had been up till then. She was losing weight and went through periods where she was constantly thirsty, just couldn't get enough to drink. She'd consume gallons of squash. Yes, the stuff with sugar in. Eek! And was always running to the loo. One particular teacher at school told her off, thinking she was mucking about, because of the number of times in her class little Yvonne would stick her hand up and ask to go to the loo. Mum and dad were worried. They took her to the doctor three times over a period of months, each time coming back with no clear answer as to what was wrong. When your child is losing weight, in the years when they are supposed to be growing – 'failure to thrive' the medics call it – it is an alarming period for any parent. Made worse by the fact that it is not uncommon for the parents to be blamed. Which is exactly what happened to us.

When Mum came back with me from the doctor the third time, I was nine and a bit and she was herself in bits. Dad got back from work and asked what had happened. It was a locum GP who had seen us. As the family used to say, I had become so thin you could see every bone in my body – in fact, you could have played a tune on my ribcage was the black humour joke in the family years later, when looking back on this period.

You have to picture a finger wagging, inexperienced young doctor here, like a pantomime villain, telling mum off.

"You're clearly not feeding her properly," the locum had said, leaving my mum in tears at being told she was a bad parent. Dad was furious, called the surgery and demanded an appointment the next evening with Old Doc Cunningham, who, despite sounding like a character in a western, had Black Country roots as deep as ours: he had been the family doctor to our grandparents, our parents, and to Graham and me from birth.

The diagnosis

I remember it well. It was my friend's birthday party the day of the appointment, which felt so unfair, having to go see the doctor yet again. But Sharon's house was just at the back of the GP's, so I wouldn't miss the party, said Mum, who spoke to Sharon's mum and said we'd be along a little late. All good so far. Enjoy it while it lasts, as they say, as we're heading for the turning point in little Yvonne's life.

Next day, as far as I was concerned, I was in my party dress and on the way to my friend's birthday, with a quick stopover at Doc Cunningham's to be got past first. We headed in to see the doctor. I can picture him now: in his tweed suit, with a big handlebar moustache. He was quite elderly by then – when he used to come around to see my granddad at home, they'd share a dram of whisky afterwards in the parlour. 'Family doctor' in those days meant they were part of the family, having treated all the generations, been part of our coming into the world and the older ones departing. It's not like that in most of the country nowadays.

After asking me a lot of questions, he called the nurse in and I went with her to pee in a pan (an awkward thing to do; I never got the hang of it) – give a urine test. I came back in and he sat me on his lap – unheard of even in those days – and opened the bottom drawer of his desk. It was full of sweets. Doctors and even dentists usually had a supply of sweets to distract children who might need consoling after an injection or otherwise need cheering up. 'A spoonful of sugar helps the medicine go down' and all that.

He told me to take whatever I wanted. Like any nine-year- old, faced with a drawer full of sweets, I got stuck in and didn't hear what he said quietly to my parents, while I was rummaging around searching out my favourites. He whispered: "She'll not be having those any more so let her enjoy them now," apparently. As I was told years later.

He got the nurse to telephone the hospital to tell them to expect me the next day. And he told Mum and Dad they needed to take me in to Dr. Everly Jones' Paediatric Clinic in the Dudley Guest Hospital, to be there 8.30am sharp next morning. Which I wasn't really paying attention to, of course. There was a party to get to! Mum took me around the corner and I ran in to join Sharon's party. I noticed Mum go into the kitchen with Sharon's mum for a bit before she left. I found out years later she'd broken down there, sharing the news with Sharon's mum. Then she went home and wept some more. The urine test had confirmed what the doctor knew from his questions and from my symptoms: I had diabetes. The news started a journey of worry and heartache for Mum over the coming years, though she bore that inside. Mum cared deeply and had a big heart, but didn't wear it on her sleeve.

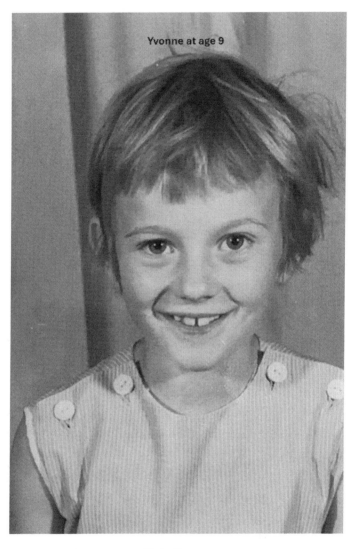

Little Yvonne

Into the hospital

The Dudley Guest Hospital. Now, you may have in your head - as a result of the word 'Guest'- a hotel-ish image. Warm and welcoming, you might think, as that's what the word 'guest' conjures up. Only it wasn't that kind of guest it was named after. It was a Victorian chain maker named Joseph Guest who took over the building, which had been built as alms houses in 1849, and converted it to a hospital that opened in 1871. Sounds a bit more Dickensian now, perhaps, shapeshifting in your mind's eye into something darker and more forbidding. "Dark, satanic mills" perhaps.

Well, it wasn't quite as bad as 'satanic', though there was the odd gargoyle up on the roof, staring down intimidatingly, as we trudged up the approach to the side outpatients' door the next morning. The main entrance was crenelated at the top, like an old red brick castle, built to keep people out. And to keep people in, as it would turn out, in my case.

If this were made into a film I guess little Yvonne, in black and white, on a dark, blustery, bitterly cold March morning, would be staring up at the scary entrance to the old Victorian institution, Mum and Dad on either side, Dad carrying a suitcase in one hand, holding Yvonne by the hand with the other, Mum doing likewise on the other side, with the innocent main character in our drama not knowing that this was where she would be living for the next three months; that Mum and Dad would be coming out without her.

Images of Oliver Twist abandoned in his Victorian orphanage might now be drifting into your mind. I don't want to encourage any sense of foreboding in you, dear reader, but the local Express and Star, when its photographer was allowed in to take pictures of the hospital after it was closed down, used this headline: "Abandoned! Eerie photos of former Dudley hospital … like the set from a Hollywood horror movie, where frights are waiting round every corner."

That's got you a bit unsettled, hasn't it. It wasn't quite as scary as the press made out, but there were ghosts in there, us kids in the children's ward were told (exactly what you want to hear at bedtime when you are nine – a ghost story based in the very building you are about to fall asleep in). And there was a Victorian taskmaster of a villain ruling with a rod of, if not iron, then a ruler of wood (and fear), inside those doors. I'll introduce you to her shortly. You might need a cushion to hide behind when she appears, as I've warned you she's scary, so get one ready.

Now, I don't want you picturing a downtrodden little thing, like a bullied Oliver Twist, entering the giant doors of this old Victorian institution and jumping as they slam shut behind. Stop biting your nails with worry and remember that little Yvonne was to become an adventurer in life. And this was her training ground for that; her first real adventure. If you discount some of the earlier ones like being blindfolded and tied to the wheel of a trike and flung down a hill, which you'll recall from the last chapter, that is. She was a resilient little thing, in other words. One that was to be tested, yes, but if you have to have a Victorian institution image in your head think of *Little Orphan Annie* – where she was an indomitable heroine in the middle of what might be miserable surroundings but she didn't allow them to be – or those resourceful kids in *A Series of Unfortunate Events*, if you're familiar with that film. Or even the smart and brave little heroine at the centre of Roald Dahl's *BFG* book and film, if you know that one. The plucky little heroine as a bright light who cheers up the dismal Victorian surroundings of the story, that kind of thing.

Though that wasn't really me as I was led into the hospital. I was in a hyperglycaemic state – my blood sugars were extremely high. I was still aware and OK; if I'd have remained untreated for a few more days, I know now I'd probably have gone into a state of near-collapse. So, it's good they caught it when they did. I'd never ventured into a hospital in my life. And so, there was this little girl, with eyes like dish plates, just taking it all in. I was in awe really, more than frightened.

We went first into the outpatient's department. I remember sitting in a huge, hall-like room, waiting to be called into yet another room. When I entered, there was a very tall, thin man: remember Christopher Lee in those old Hammer horror films? No, I'm just playing with you now. Dr Everly Jones was a very nice man, who seemed to little Yvonne, as she peered up at him, to be about seven foot tall and wreathed in clouds up there at the summit of his head, he was that high. He was a gentleman who didn't say much, but you knew he was in control and wouldn't want to do anything to upset him. Quiet authority I think is the phrase. He was accompanied by a nurse in a light blue uniform. They talked to Mum and Dad for what seemed like ages. I remember them saying, "Don't worry. She'll be fine. Have you brought her things?"

If I didn't know I was staying before this, it was beginning to dawn on our heroine now. I mean, I obviously knew on one level, as we had brought a suitcase and all the way along the cold, monolithic, mile-long marble corridors we trekked down as we went from room to room, deeper into the labyrinth, Mum and Dad kept making soothing, reassuring little noises: "It'll all be fine," "You won't be here long," that kind of thing. But the surroundings were so novel and overpowering in scale none of the words were really sinking in. Mum was probably more frightened on my behalf than me, knowing her.

There was a bit more initiation to get through first: I was taken to yet another room, where I was sat in a huge red leather chair with an arm rest. A band made of some material was put around my arm and held there on the arm rest with big metal clips. Are you starting to get scared yet? I was a bit nervous at this point, I must admit. (Trigger alert: if you don't like needles, you might want to skip ahead to the next paragraph. Little Yvonne, being in the story, didn't have that option, unfortunately).

Dad held my hand and tried to make me laugh to distract me from what came next. Which was a man in a white coat, who appeared with a huge - I mean HUGE (they didn't muck about in those days when it came to injections) metal syringe and needle. Now, I wasn't going to act scared in front of my dad, who was doing his best comedy act to keep my attention on him, but you can imagine how everything seemed to move in slow motion as that giant needle headed towards me, was placed in the bend of my arm and then in it went. And it stayed there for what felt like ages, as my very life's blood was being drawn out into it!

OK, I think that's dramatic enough for now. But you do need to get used to the fact, if you're going to stick with me throughout this book, that little Yvonne was going to be stuck and prodded with needles regularly after this first one, for ever more. It was the start of literally thousands to come over the years. There was no pricking the tip of your fingers with a tiny needle in those days to test your blood sugar levels, which was my routine in later years. There was blood taken from you – huge needle, remember - every day, or every other day if you were lucky, by the pathology people who would come around to do it relentlessly for the three months that I was there and for every routine check up thereafter. When Hollywood made a zombie movie decades later and filmed it in the (by then empty) Guest Hospital (yes, that's how welcoming and warm an environment it was - Hollywood thought it was a perfect setting for a horror film), it would have been more accurate to make it a vampire film, considering how much blood they took from little Yvonne over those three months!

Next, I was taken on a mega-walk through a maze of echoing hospital corridors to the E M Mallows Ward, where I was to live for the next quarter of a year. This was the start of the rest of my life, in a very real sense. For those Black Country locals who know the building and want to place the ward, it was at the far end of the hospital. In the bowels, you might say. Much harder to escape from, in other words, should you have a mind to. After endless corridor, you eventually came to an area that resembled the Round Room of the Birmingham Museum and Art Gallery – ornate and imposing. On the left were two huge mahogany doors to the operating theatres and on the right, equivalent doors leading to the Children's ward, both with a little porthole window in each door. It's amazing how you remember these little details, isn't it.

Mum, Dad & little Yvonne
going into hospital

We went through the swing doors, walked down what seemed like a mile-long corridor to an office at the end to be greeted by Sister Paddy, the Ward Sister.

Sister Paddy sounds quite friendly, doesn't it. A friendly little Irish lady fussing over the children you might think.

Sorry to disappoint you and your hopes for little Yvonne, but Sister Paddy was formal, strict and formidable. She wasn't the disciplinarian villain of this part of our story: every Victorian- type institution needs one, don't they, and ours is yet to come. But she wasn't to be messed with.

Mum and Dad went into her office off the ward, while I was taken into the ward on the left. We stopped at a bed on the right, by the door, which was to be my home, so to speak, for the next three months. They pulled a curtain screen on wheels around the bed. A nurse undressed me, put me in a hospital night gown and got me into bed. So far so strange! It was about to get stranger and even more Dickensian. Because, as she took the curtains away, I was faced with a sea of nine inquisitive little faces. All that was missing was the Artful Dodger. For, they were all boys. I was, it turned out, the only girl in the ward.

It wasn't like children's wards today – all soft cushions, play areas and cartoons on the walls. I remember a lot of iron about, forming a hard environment, literally: The beds were iron, with iron-railed head and footrests (not that the kids' feet would ever reach that far). When I'd been there a while and I was allowed to walk through the baby ward next door to get to the Sluice (where I had to do my urine tests several times a day), I peered up at them in their little iron cots. They seemed so high above me, poor little things, like birds suspended in cages.

Back to my arrival: Mum and Dad came in to kiss me goodbye before being ushered out. "See you later," I heard as they disappeared out of the ward. "We'll be back later. Don't worry. You're going to be fine." That's the point at which the penny dropped and I did feel sad and a bit lost. Up till then the adventure of the whole thing had been the main feeling. In those days, the sheet and blankets on the bed used to be drawn tight across the patient and jammed under the mattress on either side. In theory, particularly with children, this was to stop you falling out. In practice there was a military-like demand in hospitals for the beds to look neat and clean ('hospital corners' and all that). The effect was to trap the patient in place, held tight by the bedclothes. So, can you picture little Yvonne, head peeping out, arms trapped down by her sides, just a child shape under the bedclothes like a sardine stuck in a tin? As a result, I couldn't get up and see them out down the corridor. The staff weren't touchy feely in those days, even with children, so there was no consoling hug or fussing from an empathetic nurse to distract me. I didn't cry or break down or anything like that. I trusted them when Mum and Dad said I'd be OK and they'd be back soon. But, yes, a bit of sadness and trepidation crept in then, as they disappeared out the door. I knew no-one there; for the first time in my life, I was on my own Something happened that actually helped distract me from missing my parents, my brother and that feeling of aloneness. Or at least helped me deal with it. There was one other girl there, who was being discharged when I arrived on the ward.

She was older than me, maybe thirteen or so. She walked over to the bed. Swaggered, in fact. As she approached I thought she looked as if she owned the place. No smile. Just an aggressive look to her. She demanded, really rough and ready, "So, what are you in for?"

I said I wasn't sure. She said "Well, I think you're here for the same reason as me. You're a diabetic. You're going to spend the rest of your life here and you're going to hate it. It's horrible."

Then she said, to rub in the fact that I was stuck there and she wasn't: "I'm going now," and turned around to stalk off. Can you imagine it! Her mum heard what the girl said and told her off: "What did you say? You shouldn't say that! That's very naughty!"

I looked at her as she marched out, being scolded mildly by her mum. I'll never forget that moment. I

60

thought: "No, I will not have a horrible experience. That is NOT going to happen. It's going to be fine." She'd got my back up. That was one of the early emergences of stubborn little Yvonne who set her mind against something and was steely in her resolve. Just when I needed her to come out, she put in an appearance. As an aside, I saw that girl later for years at outpatient appointments. She was always in and out of hospital. I hardly ever was; just for routine appointments.

Being told by this girl that "You're in for diabetes and you're going to hate it," was the first appearance in my head of 'the thing inside' that you could either dread or love. This angry girl who tried to be mean to me clearly hated her diabetes, resented it, refused to look after it, and ended up constantly in and out of hospital, paying the consequences, I guess. I'd learned from a loving family that if you give love to someone, you open their capacity for love. I didn't consciously think this, because I was only a little girl, of course. But, I embraced the diabetes, determined to learn how to look after her - she became a person, someone who could be my best friend or worst enemy. I resolved she would be my best friend. Because I would be hers. I'd look after her and never neglect her. I'd love her. And she, in turn, would keep me safe. She'd warn me when I wasn't looking after us, let me and mine know that my sugars were too low or too high. Sometimes it would be a snarly warning, because she'd be alerting us to danger, having to grab our attention so that we acted fast to protect both her and me before it was too late. No room for politeness. Perhaps the greatest, most demanding challenges in life are to turn enemies into friends. Better to never let them be the enemy in the first place, but to hold them close, smother them with love and attention and they, in turn, will keep you safe. So, I owe that angry girl who tried to upset me, to make me feel as bad as she felt, a thank you for the emergence - vague and ill-defined at first in my head - and gradual formation of my FBF, my Forever Best Friend.

I've often looked back and thought if she had been softer, maybe supportive: "Hope you get on alright," kind of thing, or if she hadn't been there at all, it might have gone the other way. I might have broken down and started crying. Rather than being stoic about it. She brought out a strength that might not otherwise have surfaced. So, I look back and thank her. She'd helped me, though that was the opposite of her intentions. For those of you who may face or have faced something similar, I wasn't a little super girl back then; it could have gone either way. Even as kids (perhaps even more so as kids) we have far more resilience to draw on than we think. Particularly if you have a bit of righteous anger to call on in response to a mean provocation, like I did.

"See you later", from my parents as they disappeared out the ward door meant, it turned out, visiting hours: 2-3pm and 6-7pm every day. Mum did the afternoon session and Dad the evening, except when he was away travelling with work. (He went to work in America for three weeks at one point). The parents of the other children were lovely to me on the evenings dad could not come, especially as I was the only girl in the ward. No-one else was allowed in to visit, which meant I didn't see Graham for three months. So, no brotherly bullying. Ha ha. I did miss him. There was consolation, though: after trying to wheedle myself into his gang of mates when I was younger, only to find they didn't want a younger girl playing with them, here I was with my own gang of boys as playmates.

Though it wasn't all like a holiday camp I must add. They were to be classmates, too. There was a ward teacher who filled me with dread. A little callback here, to remind you; I did say there was a scary Victorian-like character-in-charge that we would encounter at some point. Well, here she comes with her entrance in our story, so get that cushion ready to hide behind. You thought it was Sister Paddy, didn't you. No, way scarier than her. Before she appears, and I tell you more about life in the ward, a life of learning about daily urine testing, regular blood tests, how to manage your own daily injections, how to measure out your food and adjust to a completely new diet (all of which is why I refer to this as the start of 'the rest of my life' and 'everything changed') I need to pause, as you must be thinking, "How do you cope, at nine, with being told you have diabetes? And with all that discipline you have to learn how to manage? At that young an age?"

Finding out young

Well, it wasn't that bad is the odd answer. When I think about it now, I probably felt awful to be diagnosed by Doc Cunningham as having diabetes. But I didn't really know what that meant, did I. I was more mortified that I was going to be late for my friend's birthday party. That's what's important in a nine-year-old's life, isn't it. Children, not just me, take what's in front of them and go with it. There's been research, in fact, that shows that if you find out about a life-changing illness like this when very young you cope better with it, emotionally and psychologically, than if you find out later in life. When you are older, into or past your teens, you have been programmed with what is 'normal'. And you've stopped living in the moment quite as much as small children do. You have developed a sense of a timeline to your life – a future that is being snatched away from you or changed irrevocably as much as your present by your change of circumstances. To have that sense of future taken away from you and be told you are different from everyone else is apparently much more of a shock, potentially traumatising, when it happens if you are older.

I actually think I was lucky in one way: because I was so young I didn't know any different, as they say. What I learnt over the next three months was to become my normal.

You, dear reader, get up in the morning and you clean your teeth. That's your norm. My norm as a child, learnt and normalised in me over the three months in the hospital, was to get up in the morning, brush my teeth, do a urine test, have an injection – which I learnt to do myself (with the help of two oranges; I'll explain how that happened in a bit) - and then, as the day progressed, find the time and the place for four or five more urine tests a day so you could check what was going on in your body, then organise and carry out another injection in the evening.

There's more to how my days changed in that hospital: You may eat what you want, within reason. That may be your normal. My normal was I had to learn to measure all my food - or my mum did – and what might happen to me if we got it wrong. Your normal, particularly as a child, might be to look for every opportunity to have sweet things. That's what you remember from your childhood, I'm guessing – what your favourite pudding was when you had school dinner (chocolate pudding with chocolate sauce most people say, apparently, and you can see their eyes rolling with delight at the memory when they say it, almost see them smacking their lips in recollection at the childish delight of it). And maybe there are your sweetshop favourites strong in your mind: black jacks, fruit salads, refreshers, sherbets, that kind of thing. Adults my age can list all the 1960s and 1970s brand names of chocolates and sweets that were their favourites. I learned that these treats were dangerous and could kill me if I wasn't careful. I do have fond memories of a paper triangle bag with four a penny black jacks and fruit salads in. We were allowed to go to the sweet shop on a Friday afternoon and that's what I used to choose. But that was before I went into the hospital.

But that's OK. Because I was so young, that became my norm and my routine. It wasn't like I'd lived a life to adulthood or I'd lived till my teens and then it became a real problem: I know quite a lot of diabetics that, when they find out they've become a diabetic later in life than I did, find the lurching change in their life far harder to navigate because they've become moulded, if you like, by experiencing more what it was like before – more years learning what is 'normal'- and now having to adjust away from that is such a massive mountain to climb, in their eyes, they can't imagine how they'll get to the other side; they don't want to cope with it.

The first meal I remember in the hospital still sends shivers down my spine even now, just thinking of it. On the plate was a piece of cold, white fish, mashed potato made with water and peas. As a diabetic, in those days, you weren't allowed any sauces or gravies on your food. Dad was there with me. We laughed about it years later, but at the time, he told me later, his heart sank when he saw the meal brought in as he knew I had to eat every mouthful. Because every carbohydrate in that meal was calculated according to the insulin dose I'd been given half an hour before. I think he literally spoon fed me to get every bit in. It was horrendous. The nurses were there and they were trying to encourage me, saying, "Come on Yvonne. Eat it all up and when it's suppertime you can have a glass of milk." That didn't help, because I hated milk. But there were two Rich Tea biscuits that came with the milk, so that was the light at the end of the tunnel for me. The fish went down – just about – with little Yvonne imagining the evening biscuits as her reward. Small pleasures, eh.

Before you feel too sorry for me, you have to remember that hospital meals were notoriously hard to swallow for anyone who went inside for a stay, not just me. Also, even out of hospital, food wasn't that great, to be honest, in the early 1970s. No disrespect to Mum's cooking, but English food in those days didn't give you the choice we're used to now. No nice restaurants to eat out at either.

I soon got into the routine of hospital life.

Bath time

You have to picture in your mind's eye those old roll top enamelled iron baths with curved legs, in a big, old, freezing, institutional-type, high-ceilinged bathroom. It would be an interior designer's dream nowadays; you find those baths in boutique hotels and the like. The bathrooms were at the end of a long corridor. They were windowless, just little iron grills up at the top of the wall, like a prison cell. I remember a flecked black marble floor that appeared to curve up from the floor in wings, like skirting at the bottom of the walls, to keep the floor waterproof. Everything else was all cast metal - metal sinks, metal towel rails and so on. The bathroom was so cold you'd be desperate to climb up into the enormous bath. I stood, shivering, on a wooden board and then had to be helped up to get in - it was so enormous, and I was so small. I could literally swim around in it.

Don't imagine bubbles and a relaxing spa like experience though. The soap was carbolic (I can still smell it now) and the experience was dependent on what nurse you had. Some of the nurses would let you sit in there for as long as you could (till you were a prune), others just got you in and out and that was it. So, depending on who was on duty and how warm the water was, bath times could be a nice break from the ward or a shivery affair where you were rushed in and rushed out.

Now, it wasn't all scary people in the hospital. There were angels too, hiding among the nurses. And they came out to play with us when the Sister wasn't there to see what was going on. My two favourites were Nurse Harker and Nurse Cookson. They were so much fun. We all prayed they would be on nights, as then we could have some fun. They'd come and sit on the beds and chat with us. We could shout from bed to bed to each other and have a lark. We'd all have a laugh, which was unheard of when the other nurses were on.

The Grey Lady

They'd even tell us ghost stories. Not just any old stories, but about a ghost who haunted the hospital – The Grey Lady. She was known to haunt Dudley Castle, over the road from the hospital, and was said to have lost a child in childbirth. So, she would come looking, in search of children, drawn by us and the babies' ward next door. There was a long, dark- floored marble corridor from our ward to Sister Paddy's office and, when we were all tucked up, the Nurses would tell us the story in hushed tones: that she'd been seen hovering along that corridor over the years. After reminding us of the story, they'd drop things with a clatter, make random banging noises to make us jump, leap out from behind the curtains to make us scream. Oh, it was hilarious.

It was actually clever child psychology, too. As well as entertaining us of an evening, it kept us in check. We were told that because The Grey Lady haunted the corridors at night, we must never get out of bed and leave the ward on our own. She'd lost her own child and would soon snap us up if she found us out on our own. If we needed the loo, we had to ask them, not just get up. They used to lock the huge oak doors with the little porthole in every night. That would be unheard of now. But we were glad of it then as it kept the Grey Lady out.

Staff Nurse Harker was my real favourite. She was young, beautiful and kind. I wrote to her after I left hospital and she wrote back. She went to work in London and, I found out, was marrying a guy. I was thrilled to be invited to her wedding. I was so excited that I'd see her again but blow me down, the day before the wedding my grandpa got salmonella poisoning and we couldn't go. I was heartbroken. Dad took me to her house in Tipton eventually, so I could give her the card and a little gift I'd got her. She wasn't there, after all – as it turned out I never saw her again - but her mum, dad and siblings were, and they promised to pass the card and present onto her. I do think of her and how she might be now. I hope she's OK and has had a happy life. She was a great inspiration to me; she was my Angel.

But, for every beautiful Angel like Nurse Harker, who lightens up a story, there's an evil witch. We had one of those, too. Actually, we thought of her more, us kids, as a little dragon, one who would turn up every morning and terrorise us for two and a half hours. Here comes the villain I warned you about at the top of this chapter. She was (scary timpani drum roll in the background, please) … the maths teacher! Well, not just maths, but that was the bit that particularly terrorised me.

She had silvery white, curly hair. She was even smaller than me, maybe four foot eight or so. She always wore the same grey suit and black kitten heels. She'd clip clop down the ward with a ruler in her hand – all the best villains carry a weapon to scare you with – and would rap it on your bedside table if you weren't concentrating or were doing something you shouldn't.

Every morning you'd hear the 'click, click, click' down the corridor: here she comes! And your heart would sink knowing she'd be through that door any second. She wasn't a helpful teacher: just set the work and then glared at you, marching up and down while you did it.

We'd be trying to make each other laugh, having a hoot while her back was turned, then looking all serious when she passed us. I think she is where I got my hatred of maths from, as I'd panic and make up all the answers while she was bearing down on me.

71

They'd all be wrong, and I'd constantly be in her bad books for it.

The other scary apparition who appeared on the ward even earlier than the teacher was the ward matron, doing her rounds at eight o'clock sharp. It was more the nurses on duty that were terrified than us by this particular early morning visitation. It was a bit like a Sergeant Major inspecting his troops. She was small, too, wore a grey matron's uniform with long white forearm cuffs – very Victorian – and the most enormous, frilly white hat you could imagine. It was theatrical, her outfit, if you can picture it; very scary.

We kids had to sit bolt upright in our beds, pillows behind us, and not move for the inspection. As the matron and her entourage came in through the doors, we'd freeze. Just before she appeared, the nurses would do this clever wipe movement with their hands along each bed, 'de-creasing', so everything looked smooth and spotless. Then they'd stand there like soldiers facing forward as the matron swept through. It was the nurses who'd be in trouble if anything was wrong, but their terror was infectious. After her inspection, the matron would head into Sister Paddy's office and lay down the law about what needed doing that day and what may not have been acceptable about her fly-through inspection. I could swear she flashed me a little half-smile once as she passed the end of my bed. But that was the only sign in three months I ever saw that she was human.

I've got to say I learnt a lot from those days because the ward was always spotless. Woe betides the nurses on duty, though, if there was even a cup out of place on those rounds!

There were more welcome visitors than the scary morning visitations. Once the Aston Villa football team visited, with two of the star footballers sitting in with us for a spell and chatting to the lads. The Express and Star came to document the occasion; we had our photo taken and there we were in the papers. I still have the cutting upstairs. I wasn't that interested in the football, but the sense of occasion and having the press there made it really exciting. I hadn't seen my brother for three months by then and he was not best pleased as he would have loved to have met them. He'd have been SO mad at missing them if it had been his team, Wolves (Villa's rivals). Even so, when I got home he wanted to hear chapter and verse – who was there, what did they say and the like. I couldn't remember and he was not best pleased at having no inside goss he could share with his mates. I wasn't in his good books.

When dad had to go away to America for work, he brought us back presents and he never treated Graham or I differently because that was his way. He brought me back the most beautiful 'dressing table doll', as I called it, and a furry green gonk with batteries that made the gonk laugh. When he brought them into the ward, the lads weren't bothered about the doll, as you can imagine, but they loved the gonk. In those days, you weren't allowed to keep anything brought in from outside because of infection control. You couldn't put anything in your lockers except for your clothes. So, Dad had to take the doll home. But … I kept the gonk hidden in my locker, wrapped in my dressing gown. When we had the nice night nurses on, we'd bring it out and have a laugh. At other times, the boys would egg me on: "Get your dressing gown gonk out; go on!"

Troublemakers!

He brought back walkie talkies for Graham from the same trip. These were unheard of in Britain at the time. So much so that they were held up at customs for a long time while they investigated them. Dad's plan was that, because Graham wasn't allowed in to see me, Dad could park him in the car down in the carpark, which was below the day room window. Graham would have one walkie talkie down there and I'd be able to talk to him from the day room with the other one. That was how thoughtful Dad was beneath that uncompromising exterior. It never worked out in practice because we could never get the things to work!

Another highlight of those 3 months was a secret visit from my Aunty Marge and Uncle Tony. I'll explain the 'secret' – it involved shenanigans-in a minute. I was very close to them.

Every other Saturday we would go their house and, alternately, they would come to us. They had a sweet shop in Brierley Hill. I know. I sometimes think of the irony that we had a family history of running sweet shops and yet there was I with diabetes. Anyway, before I knew about that, on Saturday nights we could have tuppence and we used to have a triangle bag to fill with sweets and help ourselves out of the shop. But obviously once I became a diabetic, I couldn't do that. About two weeks before I went into hospital, they moved south to Hitchen. That's a hundred miles away from Dudley, all the way down in Hertfordshire. They were so worried when they heard I'd gone into hospital they made the journey to come and see me. Even now, by motorway, that journey takes two hours. Yet, they wouldn't let them in after travelling all that way to see me! We're a resourceful family, however: Aunty Marge dealt with formidable Sister Paddy, talking to her in the office, keeping her sidelined. While she did that, Uncle Tony snuck into the ward and gave me a big hug and a kiss. He got told off by the nurses on duty. Kind of. "Either get out quick or hide under the bed," I remember them saying to him. He gave me a last hug, crept out the heavy oak doors with the porthole in, gave me one last cheery wave, and they were off back down to Hitchen. To this day, I don't think Sister Paddy had any idea of what happened. But, oh, did it give me a lift and a warm glow. I'm still smiling remembering it today. Martin, their son, was the one who got married to Nicky at Woolwich

Barracks - I was their bridesmaid and Graham his best man. I am Godmother to their daughter and Graham Godfather to their son and my Dad was Godfather to Martin: family ties or what! Aunty M & Uncle T brought me my first and only dog, Dylan, a huge loveable brute, and we had our first ever holiday abroad two years after I was diagnosed; so many stories from that trip, but another time maybe!

Other scary stuff happened

If you've got an image in your head of children being experimented on in a horror movie – jabbed, sucked dry of blood, fed a meagre diet, deprived of loving family – well, there was a whiff of that hanging around the hospital experience. Because, to get me used to coping with a hypo (not enough sugar in my blood) or a hyperglycaemic (too much sugar) episode, they had to induce the most dangerous situations I would face out in the world on my own and train me in how to deal with them.

My first experience of a hypoglycaemic attack was when they put me into an induced hypo so that I could start to understand the feelings, notice them as they were coming on. You tend not to have much memory of hypos. But one morning, second month into my stay, they induced one. It was scary stuff. Though not to the boys in the ward, as you will see. My blood sugars dropped through the floor and I started shouting, screaming and thrashing around. The lads thought it was hilarious; they said afterwards I was putting on a good show for them apparently. The nurses came running and pulled the screens around me for a bit of privacy, shooing my audience away.

They brought my sugar levels back up to normal with a sweet drink and biscuits – my reward for going through the bit of torture they'd had to inflict on me - and I became conscious and aware of what was around me again. I wasn't angry, resentful, scared, anything like that. I just accepted it. Looking back now I find it more scary than little Yvonne did! But, those childhood trials, tribulations and tests, whatever you want to call them, that I had to go through in that hospital became the shaper of me and who I became. If I hadn't been diagnosed young – and, again, I feel lucky to have been and for what I learned in hospital about how to handle life's challenges – it could have been so different, *I* could have ended up so different.

I remember Sister Paddy standing by the bed and talking to me about all the feelings I'd had in my body in the build up to the hypo. "So that you'll recognise one coming on, Yvonne," she said. "If you ever feel like this in future, you know what you have to do." In those days, I was taught that I needed to have two cubes of sugar followed by a rich tea biscuit. She said, "You must always carry cubes of sugar around with you."

That led to a funny constant preoccupation, for anyone not familiar with diabetes, because for years after that in every bag I'd got with me, Mum would make sure there were a couple of biscuits wrapped up in there, and some sugar cubes. I was taught, and it was passed onto Mum and Dad, not to put the sugar in hot tea because you might scald your mouth. So, you had to rub it on your teeth or your lips. Dad developed a minor pilfering habit as a result. Whenever we were out in a Wimpy bar, which was one of the rare places you'd find those little packs of two cubes of sugar in wrappers, he'd put them in his pocket. We stockpiled them. If they experienced a mysterious sugar cube shortage in the Wimpy bars in and around Dudley in the 1970s, it was down to us.

Three months of training

My three months inside Dudley Guest Hospital were really three months of intensive training in how to manage diabetes independently for the rest of my life. Several times a day, I'd be taken down to the sluice room (where all the sterilising and cleaning equipment was) to do my own urine tests – after they'd shown me a few times how to do it – with a little test tube, *clinitest* tablets and a dropper. I've still got one of those old test kits in a drawer somewhere. I'd had weeks of that, plus all the training in how to manage my food during the day, measured against the level of insulin I was given each morning. Plus, the shock training of being induced into diabetic emergency states so I could recognise them coming. Then there was all the other 'done to' daily routines – the blood constantly taken, the daily injections with insulin administered in my thigh each morning and evening. The need to be aware of how long since you've eaten and drunk, how much, and how much you need to consume later, and at what time, to stay healthy, to keep your blood sugars at the right balance.

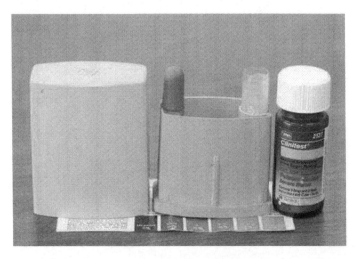

Clinitest Urine testing Kit

I was a veteran, ready to graduate into the outside world equipped to manage my life-threatening condition (hopefully) with a powerful combination of daily tools and habits that looked boringly, from the outside, like abstinence, constant time and attention-consuming preparation and planning, routine and discipline. Not a natural combination in a fun- loving, adventurous, creative nine-year-old. But little Yvonne had a steely streak, as we have grown to understand from these pages so far, and had been taught at home, indeed inherited in her bones, the family values of honesty (you mustn't try and fool yourself as a diabetic; cheating can be fatal), hard work and following routine when there was a good reason to, as much as an inner part of her wanted to kick against it.

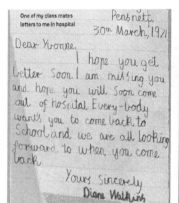

One of my class mates letters to me in hospital

Pensnett.
30th March, 1971

Dear Yvonne,

I hope you get better soon. I am missing you and hope you will soon come out of hospital. Every-body wants you to come back to school and we are all looking forward to when you come back.

Yours sincerely
Diane Watkins

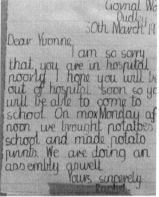

Gornal Wo Dudley
30th March 19

Dear Yvonne,

I am so sorry that you are in hospital poorly. I hope you will be out of hospital soon so you will be able to come to school. On Monday af noon we brought potatoes school and made potato prints. We are doing an assembly as well.

Yours sincerely
Rachel.

Strange and wondrous gifts

But there was one thing that I hadn't done. And it wasn't until the morning that I was due to go home that Sister Paddy walked in with two oranges to teach me how to do it. There sat the fruit, oddly, alongside two glass syringes, metal needles, an antiseptic wipe and a cotton wool ball in the kidney shaped metal tray she was carrying.

"Right, Yvonne. It's your turn to be nurse today," said Sister Paddy. Well, she knew that would work for me. I was in the game, in the moment: 'Wow, I'm going to be like a nurse.' She showed me how to draw up the insulin out of the little bottle into the syringe, then how to knock it to get the bubbles out. She passed a syringe over to me and made me do it. Then she made me do it again, about six or seven times.

I don't want to over-dramatise here, but it's simply a fact: accidentally inject an air bubble into your veins and you can kill yourself. Or at least cause a serious and potentially fatal condition – a stroke or a heart attack – if the air gets to your heart as an embolism. The idea, rare in most people's minds, that we walk a thin line every day between life and death ... well, it's something people with diabetes have to be aware of every day. We don't have the luxury of practising denial and not looking at that uncomfortable fact. And the line we walk is a narrower, more slippery one than most people. We're closer to the edge.

OK, scary glimpse into the abyss over. I don't want to suck all the joy out of this book for you as a reader. Because, believe me, my life has been full of joy, despite living near that edge. Keeping yourself away from it every day enhances how much you appreciate life and the people around you. The paradox is that there is a strange gift buried inside living with diabetes, like Hope lurking in the bottom of Pandora's box. Being aware of mortality more than most people gives you an oddly life- enhancing perspective.

Back to the fun with oranges. Sister Paddy picked one up, waved it at me and said, "Right, you're going to pretend this is going into your leg now. Hold the orange firmly, pinch it, slide the injection in." Sister Paddy and trainee Nurse Yvonne did that about four or five times, each with our own orange.

And then she said, "Right, it's your turn to be your own nurse now. Do it all again. But for real. I'll watch you. You pretend you're the nurse …"

I froze for a second. She took my hand holding the needle and gently guided it down to rest on my leg. And that's where it stopped, sitting there on the surface, me staring at it. "Go on, Yvonne, just a little push," she said. "That's all you've got to do." I felt a knock at my elbow and the needle went in. I gasped. Then she said, matter of factly, "Right, press the plunger and pull it out. Here's the cotton wool to press on it when it's out."

And I did it. And she said, "That's it. You're away. You're going home today." That was indeed it, that one session. She never showed Mum or Dad how to do it, either earlier in my stay or later that day when they came to pick me up to go home. That night, they were great - it must have been scary for them. Mum sat behind me in my room and said, "Come on, Yvonne, you've got to show us how you do an injection, so we know how it works." They may even have called Graham in as well and said, "Graham, come and see this." I can't quite recall. I never looked back. Not once did my parents ever do my daily injection. I did it myself. Thousands of times. Twice a day. From the age of nine.

I do wonder why it was done that way – left to the last day, with no formal instruction for my parents as back up. Was that approach peculiar to me, because Sister Paddy somehow judged me able to cope with it, with just one session of doing it myself ? Or did they do it to all the kids when they left? It feels a high-risk strategy, looking back. But I have learned since that other diabetic children, who have grown up with their parents doing their injections, are really reluctant to take it on when the parents try and pass it to them to do themselves. It is, commonly, a real struggle to get children who are used to their parents doing it to take the responsibility and become independent. In a sense, then, I was given the gift of a flying start.

Hold on. I hear a knocking on the wall from big brother Graham's room way back then. Or the grown up version of Graham going back in time to relive what it was like when I was in hospital and then when I came home. He has some memories he wants to share, says mine need filling out a bit, that I'm glossing over some things, that the other child in the house wants a word about, there were things I didn't know. OK. I'll hand over to my big brother for a few paragraphs, with a little trepidation ...

Graham speaks

"It's 52 years since it all began with the first diagnosis of 'Little Vonny's' condition. Some memories have inevitably faded. Others are seared into the subconscious.

I recall images of my little sister as very thin, pale and gaunt but with a big cheeky grin. Little did we know how her health was rapidly deteriorating towards a medical cliff edge which would have life changing consequences and the start of a personal journey which would define her.

I remember the utter devastation and despair of Mum and Dad who were stunned, dazed and desperate for information to understand of the condition and how they would be able to provide the care required by their precious daughter.

My little sister was suddenly taken from the family. I was constantly at our Grandparents, friends and relatives while Mum and Dad spent many hours at her hospital bedside.

Hospital visits were not allowed. The only contact was a brief exchange of waves between the hospital car park and her first floor hospital window.

I am sure that I must have written her notes, short letters or even sent her drawings, but sadly these memories have evaporated in the mists of time.

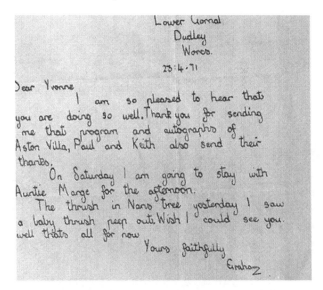

Big brother's letter to Yvonne when in hospital

The hospital stay seemed never-ending - the child's perspective of time when school summer holidays seem to last forever.

Then she was home. Hooray! All would be back to normal. But the enormity of the restrictions and the requirements that came with the condition soon became clear, even to me, a child with a naïve incomprehension of the frailties of health.

I remember:

Mum and Dad supervising Yvonne practising hypodermic inoculations on oranges.

The fridge full of little glass vials of this substance called insulin.

Meal preparations taking two hours while food was carefully weighed sugar, carbohydrate, starch, vitamin contents carefully assessed and discussed at length.

Catching Mum having a quite weep when she thought no one was noticing, having been overwhelmed by the enormity of it all.

Then there were the terrifying hypo's in the middle of the night, me cowering under the sheets in my bed while listening to my little sis shouting and screaming, with Mum and Dad frantically trying to bring her back from a diabetic hypo.

There were no upsides. Well maybe one. At least I got to eat all the chocolate and sweets.

Despite me and mine moving to the Lake District over 30 years ago, our relationship remains as strong as ever. We have developed strong enduring ties between our respective families which is a testament in no small part to Yvonne's enduring love of and commitment to family and a strong desire and willpower to ensure that she has never been defined by her condition."

Oh my! He never told me any of that at the time. Yes, it's me back again, steering the story, after that peek into what diabetes can do to the life of siblings, too. Love you, big brother. I must also say, our children, Richard, Michael (Graham's two), Harriet, Thomas (our two), and their respective partners Beth, Lizzie, Ally, and of course whoever Thomas's future Belle will be, are as close. We all party, holiday and continue to form such wonderful memories and they all work to understand the diabetes dynamics, supporting Harriet and Thomas and their Aunty Yvonne, and it's as near perfect as you can get it.

I left that hospital after three months, with a number of gifts* – not just the gonk hidden in my case, the amazing experiences, the loving nurses I idolised, like Nurse Harker, the adventures I'd been through, but the routine, the skills, the confidence, the knowledge to manage this dangerous thing that I lived with. Every day. Imagine SAS training for tiny people that need to learn how to manage a dangerous environment and you get the idea. After the three months of intensive training in how to manage her illness, it was a different little girl that emerged from her first adventure in life, headed back home and back to school.

*"In 2016, the derelict and overgrown former Dudley Guest Hospital site caught the eye of filmmakers and featured in the critically acclaimed horror movie, The Girl with all the Gifts, which starred Glenn Close and Gemma Arterton." – Express and Star.

I don't think the girl with all the gifts was based on little Yvonne. But you never know ...

CHAPTER 3

SCHOOL DAYS

The tracks of these years
Oh, so many to choose from: Manfred Man, Thin Lizzy, Led Zeppelin, Deep Purple, Paul Simon, Art Garfunkel, Slade (local boys), Rod Stewart, Barbra Streisand, Fleetwood Mac, Diana Ross, the list goes on.

My brother and I saved our pocket money to buy records.. We would go to Stantons, the local music shop in Dudley on a Saturday. I remember having my first little cassette player. Oh, and a battery-operated record player – a little green and white one that played singles. But then my close friend Suzanne, who lived down the road, provided a big step up in my musical listening experience. Her dad had an electrical shop in Dudley and a wonderful front room with state-of-the-art sound system. She introduced me to David Bowie, T Rex, reggae, fashion and make-up (I love Sue; some friends are so influential – they help mould us - and I'm so glad to still know her). Sue even took me on my first bus ride to Dudley with my pocket money to Etams (the then teenage boutique fashion store). Even now, she's got vinyl versions of every Top 20 singles of the 70's. We used to sit in their front room and listen to them and chat and dream. Then we'd watch them on Top of The Pops on TV on a Thursday evening. I'm still friends with Sue now. She's still got that collection. And yesterday. I saw her dad, as he came to my step-mum's 90th birthday party; he still lives in the same crescent. But I digress. Back to Yvonne coming out of hospital ...

* * *

Thinking of that little green and white record player reminds me of what Dad and Mum did to my bedroom when I came home. As the younger child, I always had the box room. My big brother had the bigger room. But they were determined to turn that box room into something special for me, my own little princess castle room, in fact. They said, "You can have it decorated how you want." Then I think they wish they'd never said that. Because I went for a bright blue carpet, plus - I can see them now - the 1970s-style wallpaper with symmetrical rows of bright yellow circles. Dad could turn his hand to anything and made me built-in wardrobes with a bookcase above my bed because I loved reading. And he built a little heart shaped dressing table which my mom made the curtains for - they were on a track that went around it -

and a little shelf measured exactly to fit the record player.

Now, obviously, these were great acts of parental love, turning my box room into a bijou 1970s designer pad, created to my own design. But there was a tacit acknowledgement underlying the creation of somewhere so lovely, just for me, that I would want to stay in it rather than go out. The days of going down to the woods with friends were gone, was the implication. Now, I know you grow out of that anyway, the time of exploring and playing outside, but I think their need for me to stick close to home rankled a little. The sense of a loss of independence helped fuel my rebellious streak, looking back. I still wanted to go out and do things. Just more grown- up things than I used to do.

Like going to see Swan Lake. Which is our next turning point in life. It may sound funny to describe NOT doing something as a landmark moment in the memory or in life's journey. But not getting to see Swan Lake was that for me. Let me explain …

The Swan Lake incident

A year after I'd been diagnosed, I went into Mrs Flavell's class. She fell into that category, for me, of the inspirational teacher, the one teacher that stands out in your memory. We all have one, I hope. She was class: formal, smart but empathetic and understanding. She was one of my role models in life, in fact.

We were studying Swan Lake and our art project as a class was all about creating a Swan Lake frieze for the classroom wall. I was in my element. It got even better when one morning Mrs Flavell came in and told us we were going to Birmingham Town Hall to see Swan Lake for ourselves. I was ecstatic.

We were due to go on a Tuesday evening. The coach was arranged. Going out of Gornal, for me, the girl who loved adventuring but whose scope for doing so had received the recent minor setback of being diagnosed with Type 1 diabetes, was unheard of. I was so excited. Mum and Dad had to speak to the headmaster about my evening injection, so that someone could take responsibility for me while we were there. Even though I always did them myself. That was where the happy picture in my head of what came next started to crumble to dust. The school could not support that, said the Head. Too risky. I couldn't go.

I was devastated.

Two things happened then. One was that Dad and Mum said, to stop me missing out, "It's fine. We'll go together, just us; a family outing." To their surprise, and a bit to mine, I refused point blank. I'd been, in today's terms, discriminated against, and I wasn't going to have it 'fixed' for me with a family trip. That's the way I saw it. Dad saw it differently. I was cutting off my own nose to spite my face. I was bloody-minded. I was stubborn. It was the first inkling of my 'black sheep of the family' persona emerging, as my will came up against Dad's iron will and didn't back down. He wasn't best happy with me, to say the least.

The second thing that happened – after the class had all gone and enjoyed Swan Lake and couldn't stop prattling on about it. Oops, sorry. Angry? Moi? You betcha. But the thing is, I channelled it. Which is the second thing I'm talking about.

We were all making our pieces for the frieze, still. I noticed all the models of swan ballerinas the others were making were flat. I had a brainwave: my wings had been clipped, but my piece of art would fly. Right out of the wall. Well, kind of. I went home and said, urgently: "Mum, I want some of that white netting material. Have you got any please, Mum?" I used it to make the tulle skirt of my swan ballerina that I was creating to reach right out. All the others were flat. Mine was crafted in three dimensions. I poured everything into it. Mrs Flavell, I'm sure, knew what I was up to when I took the result into class. My ballerina had earned her place in the middle of the frieze, as its focal point. She took it and stuck it up there in star position, in all its 3D glory. The girl who wasn't allowed to see it brought to life had made her own piece of art that burst out of the classroom wall, taking centre stage where its creator hadn't even been allowed to see the stage. If I had to be different and wasn't allowed to go, my piece of the communal artwork was going to stand out and be different, too. Well, you find your triumphs where you can, don't you.

That experience taught me you can channel your frustration and anger at unfair treatment and use it as fuel. A bit of righteous indignation can take you a long way. Mrs Flavell cemented herself in my mind as brilliant by that incident. I knew she would have taken responsibility for my care on the trip, but the Head made those decisions. She also taught me how to cook. I remember when I was eleven, I cooked my first Christmas cake and she stayed till 5pm to allow me to finish my icing. Although I say it myself it was fab. I cooked a cake every year after for years. Thank you, Mrs Flavell. You were a very special teacher. It's the people who see something in you, who make time for you, who put themselves out for you, who are the inspiring ones. I hope I learnt from her to try and do that in my own career later.

Mrs Flavell also gave me some grounding for my unlikely career choice not (yet) taken – playing the saxophone. She taught us recorder. And she encouraged me in it, putting me forward to play the treble and the tenor – more complex instruments than the humble basic recorder many of us have a go with at school. We had a pretty good recorder group, and thanks partly to Mrs Flavell's encouragement, I was part of it. We were so good, in fact, that we ended up playing a daytime performance at Birmingham Town Hall, the venue I'd been denied a right to go to for Swan Lake. So, I got there in the end.

As a footnote, in senior school I was back there again. Our RE teacher then, was friends with Cliff Richard (now Sir Cliff), the famous singer, through church. Our teacher was one of those enthusiastic 'go getter' kinds who create opportunities for their students to have life-enhancing adventures they can learn from. And we've already established how much I love adventures. He asked Cliff's management if his sixth formers could be stewards, showing people to their seats at the concert. Just to give us some unpaid work experience. Now, none of us really wanted to hear Cliff Richard's music (sorry Sir Cliff) but it was great fun to be allowed to do it.

So, would the Swan Lake curse strike again? Same venue, same kind of trip – an outing for the whole class to a musical event (of a different kind, of course).

I made it yet again! I can hear you cheering from here, dear reader. I was considered old enough and experienced enough to manage my own injection. But how was I going to do that, in public, in the auditorium, with a full audience and me standing in the aisle as usher? With a bit of help from a mate who held the curtain at the sidewall while I slipped behind it and did my injection is how. I'm not a musical fan of Cliff but he was really nice to us all: he came and thanked us for being his stewards. One of the girls had recently lost her dad and he had let Cliff know. He took her out for a meal to cheer her up. He is a lovely man, in my experience.

Now the first concert I went to that I really wanted to attend for the music rather than the experience (sorry Cliff) was to see Manfred Mann at the Civic Hall, Wolverhampton I must have been 16. I went with my friends Alison, John and Ian, who had passed the Dad Test and were classed as 'ok' to accompany me. My parents were obviously wary at letting me out to something so potentially raucous and unpredictable, so routine-disrupting (and routine is everything in managing diabetes) and distracting as a real live gig!

The compromise was that Alison and I had to leave before the end. I was being picked up by my dad because they were obviously worried about me being home by a certain time. "You've got to have your injection" and all that.

And then there was Bingley Hall, Stafford, to see Thin Lizzy. I went with Graham and his friends this time. It was fantastic. But with unexpected danger waiting for us at the end (and that wasn't Graham's back giving way for having me sat on his shoulders for half the night in my white Afghan coat). When we got out of that concert, it was snowing and all the cars were stuck in the fields where we were parked. We couldn't get out.

That was an early example, for me, of how something that can be a slight inconvenience for other people can turn life- threatening for someone with diabetes, if you're not prepared. Graham, when we were younger, hadn't really been solicitous of me or cossetted me as if I was fragile or anything after the diagnosis. But this time, he was the responsible adult on the spot and he shifted into high alert to look after me: "Have you got your sugar? Have you got some biscuits? Are you going to be alright?" he checked as we sat there in the snow unable to move. Yes, to all three.

I remember the snow still falling and the fantastic backdrop of the fields and cars covered in snow and absolute chaos and mayhem, with cars going everywhere – all these young drivers sliding about. We were going to be stuck there quite a while. And obviously we'd been bouncing around at the concert, so I'd used up a lot of energy, meaning my blood sugars would be low. I do remember looking around in the hope I'd see some St John's Ambulance people there just in case we needed them. Nope. It was down to me and big brother. When I list 'routine, following rules, self-discipline' as some of the values I live my life by, I'm aware that may sound unlike the adventurous me with a sense of fun that people know.

But, in moments like being stranded at the end of that concert, you learn that you are only allowed to be spontaneous and have fun if you've done the routine and planning – the sugar cubes, the biscuits, blood glucose testing kit and the injection kit all ready for when you need them – in advance.

Do the right thing

The rest of the seventies were great. I did well at school. I had failed my 11 plus in the early seventies, with many of my friends going onto grammar school without me, but I loved my secondary school; I had great friends. It gave me my grounding for life and taught me to appreciate so much. I must also introduce you to my other long-term friend here, Jean, who I met whilst in sixth form introduced to me by another school friend Claire. She is godmother to my daughter and we have shared many memorable adventures with many more to come I am sure, but I will never forgive her for introducing my husband, who you will get to know later, to the local running club and our hours of separation, whilst introducing me to circuit training and pretend running in comparison.

In fact, I became Head Girl. Though it might only have lasted forty-five minutes and then been snatched away from me if it'd gone the wrong way. The new Head Boy (and good mate) and I had just left the school stage and headed over to the sixth form common room after being presented to the school as the new Head

Boy and Head Girl. Everyone was mucking about in there and one of the lads chucked a board rubber at us as we walked in. I leapt up and caught it and chucked it back. He ducked and it went straight through the window. A closed window, that is. It shattered completely. So how was I going to go home that evening and tell my dad what I'd done? "Oh, by the way I was made Head Girl today Dad, but it didn't last very long." Get out of that one, as they used to say back then.

I always believe in tackling things head on. So, I bit the bullet and went straight to the headmaster, Mr Firth's, office and 'fessed up. I apologised profusely. I did tell a bit of a white lie by saying it was a pencil case that had a bottle of ink in that I didn't know about and the bottle of ink had broken the window when it hit. A soft pencil case sounds a bit more innocent, doesn't it. I received a big lecture. Well, he had to, didn't he. But then came the much hoped-for, "I will overlook your mistake just this once." So, I retained my head girl ship. By the skin of my teeth.

That wasn't the only scrape I had gotten into in the 70s. Back in the sixth form I was dating an older lad. I was 16. We went into the Saracen's Head Dudley, which was Lenny Henry's regular, though I never saw him in there. We went in and sat down when something horrific happened. A guy walked in with an empty pint in his hand, marched up to a guy at a nearby table and just glassed him in the face. It was horrible, blood everywhere. Absolutely horrendous.

I was underage, but I wasn't drinking. When the police came and questioned us all, nobody would say they saw it and that they could identify who did it. Though they all knew. It was the code of silence; you don't dob into the police. I was almost as horrified by that as by the attack. When the police came to us, we told them everything. They kept me out of the witness box, but my boyfriend testified, and the guy went down. People had warned us against saying anything, telling us to keep our head down. But I was not going to stand by out of fear. I was my father's daughter, after all.

The shock of that incident affected me profoundly. And I had to do something more about it. I'd been going through the rounds of a public speaking competition for the school. Everybody thought my subject would be diabetes, for obvious reasons.

But I gave a talk on violence instead. My art teacher, whom I got on really well with, agreed to help. We used shock tactics in case there was anyone in the audience who might not realise what a brutal and unthinkable thing glassing is and might be tempted that way themselves one day. My teacher made a gigantic mural – about seven foot by six – of a face that had been glassed. And we revealed that as the backdrop when I went up to give the talk. Then I broke all the conventions. I didn't stand at the lectern. I prowled about and scared the life out of them to get them to realise what violence is really like. I'd asked the Head's permission to take a brick, a crowbar and a glass up on stage. I smashed the glass, jumped down off the stage and acted as if I was going for people in the audience. I was terrifying. But I won the speaking competition. I had to. Because there was kind of a moral imperative there for me. I think that's a theme that runs through my life: I can't see oppression or discrimination or unfairness of any kind taking place around me without standing up and doing something about it. That's what I mean when I say my school experiences helped form me. I found that speech the other day, by chance and reminisced over all the wonderful school days at Ellowes Hall.

Dudley Guest Hospital again!

Now, this memoir is in danger of becoming a mite too serious, though it is important to get in the serious things that form us and help shape our values. So, let's get back to scrapes and near-misses, to lighten the mood for you as we approach the end of this chapter. A couple of times, earlier in my school life, Dudley Guest Hospital reached out its scary hands and tried to pull me back, would you believe.

The first time was in my final year of middle school I was at my friend's house for an overnight stay. We were playing badminton and the shuttlecock landed on the garden, six feet below. I went to retrieve it, jumped down and felt a pain shoot up through my ankle. It came up swollen and bruised but I just put up with it for a week. I had a diabetes check up a week later at the Guest and hobbled in. The doctor took one look at me, said I needed it X-rayed and … it was broken. Little Yvonne must have been a tough cookie to be limping around on a broken leg for the week. I was plastered up and sent home (phew, escaped the hospital's clutches) with the slightly messy cast on. That day we'd had a new lounge carpet put in, so mum put newspaper down, so that I wouldn't walk on it! There were positives, though, to having a leg in a cast. I got to sit on a chair in assembly, ring the bell for playtime and for the beginning and end of school. And I got to come into and leave school five minutes early, to beat the rush. There's always a silver lining if you look for it.

The second time Dudley Guest called me back, so to speak, was during CSE exams. If you look at a picture of the hospital, there's a central building with a tower and a large, imposing window. That's where I sat my CSE Commerce and Economics exams. Because the week I was taking my exams I was hospitalized. They thought it was because of all the psychological pressure of exams mucking my bloods about – stress does that. So, I was dragged back in in for a week. "I can't," I said. "I've got these two exams!" They kept me in, but I still sat my exams. One of the teachers from school, Mrs Hicken, came and sat with me in the tower room. And they brought out some milk (lovely! You'll remember how much I enjoyed that last time I was there …) and two rich tea biscuits halfway through. Just like old times. . Another near miss with the Guest Hospital was when studying for my A levels, I was serving tuck in lower school (the Tuck shop I was instrumental in setting up, no less) with my mate Pete and I collapsed (low blood sugars again). Paramedics were called and the lower school were given 30 minutes extra break, I was their hero, I was checked over and back to studying I went. Ironic, I suppose; surrounded by all that tuck and collapsing for lack of sugar in my blood.

It wasn't the last time the Guest Hospital reached out its hand to me. Jumping ahead in our timeline for a moment, I actually chaired a big NHS meeting in the same room there, the board room. I had to hold it together when I walked back in, thinking, "I sat my CSEs here, a couple of decades ago, was a patient here a decade before that. Now I'm chairing this big NHS meeting in the same place. Pull yourself together, girl." I was a bit overwhelmed, to be honest, with memories flooding back.

Now it's closed, you'd think I'd be safe. But, the Guest Hospital looms up from the past and reaches out to me still, even finding its way into our lounge. Let me explain: I saw a trailer for one of those ghost hunting programmes where celebrities tour an old building in the dark. Guess which building it was. I said to Tony, "We have to watch that!" When we did, it was eerie for a whole load of extra reasons for me than it was for anyone else watching it. Christopher Biggins (the then King of the Celeb Jungle) was with other celebrities who had braved creepy crawlies in the Australian jungle and participated in fearsome bush tucker trials, but now came to face their worst nightmares by ghost hunting in the Black Country, including the Guest Hospital. There they were, running down dark, abandoned, scary corridors, with the light of the camera following them, the whole place looking derelict and forlorn. As we watched, I thought, "I know every inch of that corridor you are running down." The Grey Lady, wisely, avoided all the ruckus and didn't make an appearance.

Enough busting of the timeline: I told you I'd hop about a bit rather than stay in my lane, so to speak. Back to school. Or the end of school, which is the right place to end this chapter. The wider world beckoned. Some of those who loved me wanted me to stay close at hand, safe in my support network of family and friends. But I had other ideas. It was a tumultuous time actually, with me and Dad at loggerheads again. I didn't get the A level grades to go to my first-choice universities. He wanted me to go do a secretarial course at Worcester college, not far from home.

But I had another direction set in me that had been there for a while. I'd experienced enough of the NHS to know that as wonderful as it was, it could do with some help. I didn't want to go in on the clinical side. I wanted to help on the management side. I'd seen a lot of improvements that needed doing and wanted to be part of shaping that. But one of the few places in the country that offered a degree in business and administration for the public sector was on the other side of the country, at Teesside Polytechnic, Middlesbrough.

They offered me a place through clearing. The stage was set for a showdown with Dad. And a new adventure began.

Birmingham Town Hall

CHAPTER 4

THE UNI YEARS

TRACKS OF THESE YEARS
I had the time of my life …
I danced: *I Wanna Dance with Somebody,
Whitney Houston*

I found myself: *Take on me, Aha*

I made great friends: *Don't you forget about me,
Simple Minds*

Love came a' calling: *Tainted Love, Soft Cell*

I sang and stomped along with Come on Eileen. When that song came on at a club or disco it always raised the roof, everyone singing along. Dexys (the band, not the drugs) were so cool and there's added poignancy now to that song as I realise it refers to Johnny Ray, whom Dad loved and Eileen was my course mate.

There was so much great music as the soundtrack to my Uni years: Relax by Frankie Goes to Hollywood,

Spandau Ballet, Lionel Richie, The Three Degrees (sorry not my taste but mentioned for reasons covered later), Elvis Costello - definitely a fan, and again more on this later.)

They're all classics and have travelled through time with me instead of being left in the past because my (adult) kids love them and they are still all over Smooth Radio (or Soft Radio as I call it - I'm always getting my words mixed up) and played at parties. Whenever we're out and one of those songs from the 80s comes through the speakers, the kids turn to me and say, "That's one of yours, isn't it?" Yes, I think with a smile on my face: one of mine. Isn't it fab when your kids think your music is cool.

So, that's the soundtrack you need to imagine, along with the big shoulders, big hair, leggings and other fashion missteps of the early 80s that went with the music, as you join me for the following adventures, with the Black Country girl grown to an adult (almost) and transplanted to a shared student house in run down Teeside, Northeast England. But to me it was far from rundown; it became my home, it was where I began to find myself, my independence and my focus on the future.

* * *

Mum and Dad dropped me off at 21 King Edward Square, Middlesborough, to start my first year at

Teeside Poly. Looking up at the bleak façade of a dingy student terrace house in the cold gloom of a Teeside afternoon, I couldn't help but wonder what I'd done and how I'd got here.

I'd had to fight my way past Dad's objections, was how I'd got here. When my 'A' level results came in and they weren't good enough for where I'd wanted to go, he had thought that was a done deal: "No university for you then," he said. "Secretarial studies at Worcester College, Yvonne. Close to home; family and community all nearby, and you'll get a good career out of it." He was furious when I turned that down. Relationships became strained.

First, it was what I wanted to do that he didn't agree with: "Business and management? In the NHS? Why?" It made no sense to Dad. I tried explaining it was his influence; I wanted to take what I'd learned from him about management and apply it to helping the NHS. "If you want to manage, just go into management, then," he'd said.

But I knew what I wanted to do: apply management learning to the NHS. Then, when Teeside Poly accepted me, through clearing, for their BA (Hons) sandwich degree course in Public Administration – a business degree designed for the public sector; exactly what I wanted to do - it was a red rag to a bull: where I wanted to go was now added to the problem; the extreme northeast of the country.

Consett steelworks were not far from Teeside and Dad had been up there on business many a time.

He knew first hand how rough and rundown the area was. I know he was worried for my safety, but it didn't make it easier to weather the storm.

"It'll take five or six hours to get to you by car if we had to in an emergency, even longer by train, changing at least twice. And you've no idea what it's like there. You'll be on your own in a dangerous area." He wouldn't give up: the objections came flying at me. "How will you manage? You've got no doctors up there? How will you get your medication?" He was relentless. His daughter was putting herself at risk for reasons he didn't support, and he wasn't having it. He was fighting to defend me. Even if it was me he was fighting.

All the while, as we had these showdowns in the front room, Mum would be worrying in the background. She hated us being in conflict. And she was worried about how far away I was going.

But I stood firm. For him, this was a rerun of the stubborn, 'cut your nose off to spite your face' refusal to go to Swan Lake. I ran through his objections, countering each one. I had made all the medical arrangements with my consultants to continue after I'd moved, I'd get a GP there, and so on. I wouldn't back down.

So, I'd got what I wanted. Apart from a very disconcerted Dad and a very worried Mum, which of course made me sad.

I was the first there, a run-down terrace house overlooking a square of garden (which we were to grow to love as our sanctuary). Dad was keen to get off; now I totally understand why, as it was a long journey in one day, but I knew Mum was petrified and so held her long and hard and told her not to worry; I would phone every Tuesday. She was so worried about my diabetes. Although I had managed it for years, I'd now be hundreds of miles away, with no immediate contact and no one local yet knowing I lived with the condition.

I waved, grinning, full of life, wanting to keep things cheery. Years later, Mum shared that she cried on the way back home. Dad was not from the generation to hug and offer soft words of support. He would have said "Dot, she has made her bed, she will be fine and if not, she will have to lie in it."

I dealt with it. I had the time of my life - so many scrapes and adventures - and met and made lovely friends (plus fought off a bastard or two, of which more later: all life stories need a villain or two to be overcome along the way, don't they).

As they drove off, I had my insulin pens, urine testing kit and blood glucose machine. I was free and alive. I was eighteen and had never lived away from home before. Well, I'd wanted an adventure. Here it was. Shabby and run down it may have looked to them as they drove off. But, I absolutely loved it.

This is where I met my closest Uni friend Mo, who introduced me to the world: men, fun, drugs and drink. I never tried the drugs. We had so much fun, and she was a lovely person. Her dad was a North Yorkshire GP and the family farmed. We shared the house together and formed the hub of Uni social life in that street, which was full of student accommodation. There were two girl houses in the Square, twenty other male houses. We formed a particular bond with the guys next door and in a house diagonally opposite.

My diabetes was brilliant throughout Uni, and I now question that I lived life to the full, given the absence of diabetic mishaps, so to speak. But I promise it's true! I partied, I burnt both ends of the candle, I didn't over drink (it messes up your blood sugar and is dangerous for a diabetic) yet still had a ball. Hidden out of sight of student friends, I managed the illness, which meant juggling insulin injections and blood glucose testing in those days.

This was real undercover work. Literally. I became so adept at it that I would inject myself through my jeans, under the table, in the library, when we went for coffee or to the pub, so that none of my friends would be worried or distracted by the steps I had to take to manage my diabetes every day. I'd never go to the loo in a public place to inject as I never knew if they were clean. It was my secret life, running alongside and essential to the life lived in plain sight, like a swan's legs underwater, paddling furiously against a strong current so that, on the surface, there's a serene progression forward. Or, in my case, so that the Yvonne my friends experienced was that fun girl from the Midlands with all the get up and go, who was always up for an adventure, which is how my friends say I was. And I was. But, I couldn't have been without the discipline of the hidden life.

Still there are things that jump up and bite you in life. No matter how disciplined I was about managing the known danger. It didn't prepare me for being ambushed by a different one. It all went horribly wrong, almost confirming Dad's direst predictions. I was living the dream, learning how to spread my wings when, after just a couple of months, I was struck down, so ill I had to go home. No, not the diabetes; something else entirely.

In the December of my first year, I felt awful; I was in so much pain and my housemates were worried for me. I went to the GP I'd registered with. I can see him now: 60-ish, tweed coat, austere face.

His first words were, "Are you taking drugs?"

I said yes. He smirked.

I said, "Insulin. I am a type 1 diabetic." That wiped the smirk off.

He examined me and diagnosed shingles. There was no apology for the 'druggy student' assumption, just the slightest, barely discernible hint of sympathy as he told me I was so ill I needed to go back home to recover.

It was a Tuesday night and I stopped in the phone box on the edge of King Edward Square and phoned home. I was in so much pain, I was sitting on the floor of the phone box and only just managed to get the phone to my mouth. (In case you don't know, shingles is from the chicken pox virus that lays dormant in you from childhood but occasionally pounces in adulthood with a really painful attack that can last months). Dad said he was in Consett the following week and would pick me up early before term ended. Now I know he probably wasn't, God bless him, but also knew mum would be stressing fit to bust and that bothered me. As well as the terrible pain.

Dad turned up as promised to pick me up. We filled the car with my stuff, as that was it for me for that first term, with the help of the lads next door. They very helpfully placed two fire extinguishers from one of the houses in the back of the car, too, without Dad noticing what they'd done. Student high jinks, eh. Dad spotted them two miles down the road and went ballistic. He turned round, we ended up back in front of the house and he put the fire extinguishers back where they belonged, all the while with a face like thunder. Luckily for the boys who had 'helped' pack the car, there was not a student in sight. It was an emotionally chilly journey back. The prank had confirmed Dad's worst fears about the company I was keeping. I was still the black sheep.

Even so, for the next few years, I had an absolute blast! I met amazing friends, had a series of occasionally hairy adventures, learned how to navigate around and survive the dangerous types and places that did indeed lurk on the edges of my new home, and even had to deal with danger coming from an unexpected and supposedly safe source, from within the college. Which I will explain later.

I also learned that you can make yourself part of a community on the other side of the country and gain its support if you are open to that. We had two lovely cleaners in the house, for example, and we made friends with them. Mo and I would be up early and we'd offer them a cup of tea. They said no-one else did that. They'd then tell us where was safe to go and where to avoid. "I'm telling you as if I'm your mum, now, you don't go into this part of town at night, and you don't walk down that street," that kind of thing. They looked out for us.

I'm getting ahead of myself now. You need an introduction to Mo – my beautiful friend, Moira - one of those vitally important friends you encounter that change your life, or at least accompany you on so many adventures and experiences that you can't imagine that period of your life without them. Mo was three years above me, in her last year in fact, so knew the ropes. You could say she took me under her wing. She had the best room in the house, ground floor, at the back; perks of seniority over us first years, I guess.

I was in the lounge, meeting the other newbies who had come in after me in dribs and drabs on that first day, when in walks this larger-than-life woman, big smile on her face, but with a strong sense of 'no messing' presence. She shouted a cheery "Hi" to everyone and strode through to her room at the back. By the time she'd settled her stuff in and come back out, it was just her and me in the lounge. Mo was tall, striking, had a presence about her, bubbled with energy and warmth and confidence. I was a fan from the start. She was in her final year of a clothing retail course, focussed on the design side, so had a streak of glamour about her, too. She was my guru when we went around the charity shops – "This is you, Yvonne; you put a belt around it like that, you'll look fantastic, girl!" – so much fun to be with.

Hold on a minute. If I'm sharing with you my first impressions of Mo, it's only fair we look in the mirror (using Mo as my trusted mirror) and break authorial convention here by letting Mo describe her first impressions of me then - Yvonne, just turned 20.

Mo speaks

"It was the start of the 1980s. I heard her laughter before I even met her, ringing through the student house that Yvonne and I were to share with 11 other girls. Her personality was infectious; warm and enthusiastic, every day was an adventure in her company and we became firm friends.

She took me to my first ever football match, shouting 'Come on you Wolves' from the midst of the Middlesbrough supporters stand without caring who would hear her. My vocabulary expanded massively with all the Brummie vernacular she introduced me to.

Her powers of persuasion were legendary; I remember she ruthlessly negotiated down the price of a pair of jeans for me one day using very little more than a direct request and her amazing capacity to make others laugh.

Clever and capable, she had a gift with people. I recall never seeing her down in the mouth, her positivity and energy rubbed off on us all."

That's enough, Mo. I'm blushing now and this is my book, so I have to elbow my beautiful friend out from behind the keyboard and take over authorial ownership again. Right, I'm back in the driving seat so can reaffirm that it was Mo that led me astray and **not** the other way around, as she would have you believe in that little story of me cheering on my local team in the midst of an army of famously volatile Middlesbrough fans!

She dragged me into countless adventures I'd never have had if we hadn't met and bonded instantly. So, a couple of weeks after that first meeting, Mo says to me, "Ever played darts, Yvonne?" "Never," says I. "Well, you do now. We've a place on the student team for our next match, and you're it." She wouldn't accept any objections: "I've never picked up a dart in my life! I can't add up!" Mo breezed past all of it: "You'll be drinking pints. It's free. We'll help you do the adding up". (Of course, they didn't in the end; you're up there with the arrows having to work out the numbers as you go). "You'll have a fantastic time. Minibus is coming at 6pm. Be ready."

And I was. It was a bit of a shock, though, when the minibus took us to a working men's club in Redcar. We were playing their women's team. You didn't mess with those women; they made their men look soft. I got through it without making a fool of myself. It turned out I could throw an arrow after all. In fact, we won. And from then on, I was on the student women darts team, travelling every other week to all the seedy nightspots Dad would have had a fit about if he'd known. They were adventures all right, and some rough places, but I loved every minute. When we got back safe, from each trip out to the wilds of every rough pub and club for several miles around Middlesbrough, we'd regale the other girls in the house with our scrapes and adventures over a cup of tea. I would love to introduce you to my other flatmates throughout those years but must move on, with the exception of Lynne (my surrogate Mum, also in her final year) whilst there, who got married to a guy from next door, moved to and introduced me to the lovely Lakes where my brother set up his family home in latter years, Her hubby worked at Windscale Nuclear Plant and on one of the many weekends visiting he got us a tour, which was awesome. I would love you to be reading this Lynne and that we could get back together.

Oh, so many adventures, I can't get them all down here – there isn't enough room. So, I'll share some scenes with you as they flash across my brain. Think of it as one of those montage scenes in the middle of a movie - strung together to give you flashes of what happened. Like Rocky training for the big fight kind of thing, but with alcohol and a lot of singing and dancing and staggering home late.

In my first year, Moira's final year, we and another mate went to a fancy-dress party as The Three Degrees - in black stockings, black bin liners and black humongous wigs made from sugar paper purloined from the art department. We looked fabulous, darling.

More dressing up for you to picture; we did a fancy-dress three-legged race for charity. Mo also did a sky dive for charity (she was fearless). Well nearly - on the actual day it was postponed due to inclement weather but Mo featured in the tabloids skydiving anyway. This is how we managed it: we balanced her on a bollard outside, while the photographer from the paper lay flat on his back below, brave man. You'd never have known she wasn't skydiving!

Back down to earth, we were regulars at our local Pub, The Empire. This was part of breaking the ice in joining a new community, as it was very territorial; when we first went in and sat down, we were made unwelcome. We had innocently sat in what turned out to be the regular seats of two local characters, who turfed us out when they came in and found us there. Imagine two ladies of a certain age, glacial features, inch-thick makeup, bright red lipstick, pill box hats, couture coats and a menacing look about them. We knew our place; we moved to adjacent seats with profuse apologies and soon became accepted as locals. Middlesbrough was tough but it was a wonderful place; when you got to know the people, they cared for you.

Some adventures were a bit closer to home. I remember we'd been out to a nightclub – it was a student town so there were lots of nightclubs in the centre of Middlesbrough, like Mandy's, one of our favourite haunts – and we were coming back later than usual one night. There was me and Mo and a couple of lads from next door. Now, a mile or two down the road were the docks and we were told you never cross the line and stray over there as the docks in those days were dangerous, especially at night; really rough. The prostitutes gathered there to meet the dockworkers coming off the night shift at two or three in the morning.

So, this night, we see, across the road from us, an old docker coming off his night shift, pushing his bike. He's covered in grime from work but grinning from ear to ear. Because, on the handlebars of his bike, he's pushing this prostitute in a red dress, high heels, bright red lipsticks, the works. If we'd had a phone to take a picture … I can see them now; it'll stay in our memories for life. They're giggling and laughing with each other. They're as happy as Larry. And the old guy shouts over to us, "Had a good night, you lot?" We were fellow denizens of the night, if you like, shouting hellos across the street as we wended our way home. Talk about 'Take a walk on the wild side'.

Occasionally the wild side got a bit too close to home. We had Friday nights in the Uni Bar then everyone would troop back to ours for kebabs. You know yourself, there's nothing like a kebab after a night out; that gnawing hunger you get that only a greasy hot kebab will cure. That was our Friday night treat. But you took your life in your hands to get them. One night Dawson, a guy from next door, volunteered to go get them after we'd all got home late. He didn't want any help, he said, staggering off into the night to pick up our supper. We were starving. He was gone for ages. We weren't best pleased as we wanted our kebabs. As time passed, we got concerned for him, not just our growling stomachs. Two of the guys went out and found him trudging back, looking sheepish. He'd been mugged. Worse thing was, he was on the way back with our dozen or so kebabs and so ... the muggers had nicked our kebabs! He never lived that one down.

I need to pause the fun for a second here to reveal a bit more of the secret life that allowed this 'normal' student life to take place without killing me. I'm not being dramatic, honest. The kebab, for example, was more important to me than it was to my mates, more than just a shared indulgence with friends to round off a great night. Going out dancing, I knew, used up a lot of carbohydrates, which threw my blood sugars out of balance. I correspondingly needed to end the night with something carb-rich to make sure I had enough sugar in my bloodstream not to sink into a hypo while asleep. Because you don't always wake up from those. So, there was an underlying urgency - for me - to even a funny story like the night of the stolen kebabs.

I had to learn myself, through trial and error, because I didn't have a clue how many carbs were in a kebab. All packaging is labelled now, with all the detail you need (though it's not stamped on kebabs even now, of course). But it wasn't then. And, if you've been paying attention, Dear Reader, you'll remember (quick surprise test here for you to make sure you've been paying attention) that little Yvonne, in her two month stint in hospital, was taught how important carb counting to keep healthy, to avoid her bloods dropping too low or rising too high. And had put that into practice ever since. Because it kept her alive. As an aside, I had a school reunion years later and someone from school came up to me and said she'd wondered if I'd be there, as she'd read that a large percentage of Type One Diabetics born in the early sixties don't survive beyond thirty. They didn't. I wasn't going to join their ranks. But, I was going to enjoy a kebab like all the normal people. The first kebab made me feel lousy, as it was too carb rich and pushed my bloods sky high. I had to compensate with extra insulin. Gradually, I worked out the balance. And I recorded it all in my secret diary.

No, not that kind of secret diary. This one kept me alive. And kept me healthy. Every minute of every day, with Type One Diabetes, part of your mind is calculating: how many carbs were in my last meal or snack or pint (I was a student, remember), how long ago was that, how much insulin have I injected so far today, have I been more or less active than usual so far (sitting in the library or running around Brian Clough's park kicking a football around with my mates - see below - or dancing the night away), what and when should I eat or drink next, how much and when to keep healthy and alert, have I got something strenuous coming up so I have to load up with carbs in advance, or a night in the bar so may need less insulin than usual in advance of that to counter the effect it has on lowering your blood glucose?

Every carb of every minute and every activity went into my secret book so I could track it, along with a record of how I felt, how my body and mind were, as a result of that intake and exertion. Every Type One Diabetic had their own Secret Diary. The NHS imaginatively labels this book the Blood Glucose Monitoring Book. Not the most scintillating title for the book you write to monitor your life every day and keep a record of the information you and the healthcare professionals need to keep you alive and healthy. I adapted mine, of course, spending ages putting in columns for the readings, then working out I needed an area on the page for comments. You take the book with you to every hospital check up and it's pored over. Obviously now that's all digitised with automatic recordings. (My nickname now I have a grandson is Nanny Beep, because of all the beeps and alerts and alarms emanating from about my person). But, you had to allocate a portion of your brainpower to managing that secret life and keep that part of your brain turned on and alert all the time, from the minute you woke to the minute you fell asleep. Your life depended on it. You still have to, even now, of course, even with the arm sensor beeping for you as it constantly reads what's going on in your body. As an aside, you know me by now through these pages, and how I'm always trying to improve things (you've probably picked that up) so the hospital used to marvel at my book and say we should publish it as a template for other people with Type One, to make it easier for them to fill it in and then read things at a glance.

Someone did end up publishing one and it was very similar to the improvements I'd worked out for mine, to keep my life on track.

So, there you are, you're now privy to the secret life of the diabetic, the intensive, non-stop undercover work that went on under the table, behind the scenes, in the pages of our secret diaries, a private life constantly managing what my running companion Anne would in later years call 'Yvonne's constant companion, her Type One Diabetes, the little friend who would occasionally jump out and shout at us when we'd run too much'. Or, on one occasion, try and push Anne into a cut alongside the running route. Yes, we have to manage and contain that potential other self so that our public life can be lived and enjoyed with you normal people as the real loveable us. Ideally without you ever knowing. Back to the carefree student life that secret life of discipline enabled, with a story about a fun encounter with someone you may recognise.

We were out dancing a lot, often to live bands. In Newcastle, on a jaunt one night, we're in this tiny venue with a small stage in the corner, the dance floor right up close to the band. The lead singer clocks my mate, they exchange glances, he jumps off stage (steps off really – he was right next to us and on our level almost) and we end up dancing with him while he's still singing the song. He was far tinier than he looks on the telly; Elvis Costello (yes, we were dancing with Elvis Costello!) is not much bigger than me.

Another night you have to picture is me and Mo in the snow on a railway station platform again in Newcastle, miles away from our town, the waiting room locked (with us on the outside of it), hoping for a train that never came, huddled on a snowy bench until six o'clock the next morning. We were supposed to be staying with a mate of Mo's, but the house was minging – damp and dirty – and there'd been a bloke who was a bit too pushy and aggressive in wanting to get to know me. We did a moonlight flit on the spur of the moment. Only to find it had started to snow and there were no trains till morning.

Now, that incident was an example of an unexpected event jumping up and biting you, derailing your plans (almost literally, in this case). Stranded overnight on a snowy train platform is uncomfortable and inconvenient for most people, with the consolation that it makes a great story for years after, with its whiff of uncertainty, brush with danger, will they or won't they get home, the snow falling on us in the night, the flight from the lairy guy earlier in the evening. But, if you have diabetes, the danger is real and present. The bit of your head that always has to be prepared has made sure you've got little bottles of Lucozade and sugar biscuits and injections crammed into your bag – I tell you, that's a bulge in the bag no other girl on a big night out had to plan for and protect as if they were valuables (which they were) – else that long snowy night on the platform would have been a lot more dangerous. I was always being teased for my bulging bag, with my mates saying, "You can fit my keys in there, can't you?" Didn't exactly make for the sleek, streamlined look on a night out. So, even when living the student high life, apparently having a wonderful carefree time (which I was), I had to maintain the discipline underneath that, often hiding it from friends, to manage the diabetes all through those wild student years. It did not stop me having fun. But you couldn't ever afford a lapse in being prepared for unexpected moments like that night on the platform.

I have to share a few scenes of montage moments from my second year, because I'd moved out of the dodgy student accommodation of my first year into … even dodgier student accommodation, it turned out, with a mate, Jackie from Manchester. It was the one and only Ayresome Green Lane, a flat above a hairdresser's. Now, despite the rural sounding 'Green Lane', this was where Middlesbrough Football Club's old ground was, Ayresome Park (before moving to its flash new Riverside stadium). It was one of those old northern club grounds, in a road in the heart of the working-class community.

The day before the first matchday there, all these wooden boards suddenly appeared from inside the houses at six on a Friday evening. We stared: what was going on? What kind of weird local ritual was this? All the terraced houses along the road were sticking these heavy wooden boards up on their windows, as if preparing for a riot. Which, in a way, they were. It was, we were told, because the next day thousands of rowdy home and away fans would be charging down our road, sometimes having running fights, usually drunk as can be, and the locals had to protect their windows and hide indoors until the storm had passed. And then do it all again ninety minutes later. Our boyfriends of the time rented a house which was next door to where the famous Middlesbrough footballer and later Nottingham Forest manager Brian Clough no less had lived and we shared many an hour in his local Albert Park, also kicking a ball about but with not quite as much skill as he had displayed when he kicked one around the same park as a kid.

The cleaners – our substitute mums – warned us when they found out where we were moving to: "Never walk down that street alone at night," they said. We hardly ever did. There were students living all down the road, with us the furthest along, and the lads would walk us to our door most nights if we were coming back late.

One other scene for your montage was on a Saturday. I was working in the front room when Jackie came in and said, "You have to see this." The local blokes all had a skinful on match day and there was this guy sitting on the edge of the road, outside his house, opposite us, a bottle lolling in his hand, like one of those Victorian scenes of debauched working-class life – Gin Lane and the like. So, we're staring down through the window from the safety of our flat above the hairdresser, and his wife appears at the front door and starts berating him. He turns and lobs the bottle at her. She ducks inside, finds a couple of things to hurl back at him, does so, then shouts, "That's you out then!" and slams the door. We could hear the bolts going. He starts hammering on it, but she won't give in. So, he's out there for hours on the pavement, drunk and locked out. What a scene.

Now, we missed the street's football lockdown most weekends: my flatmate had a regular boyfriend at home in Manchester, so would be away. And Mo had moved out to live in Gisborough, a lovely little market town up the coast, to be near her new job, working for a local clothes' manufacturer. So, I'd head off to Mo's most Friday nights, safely away from football hell, on the bus, travelling with Mo's boyfriend, Mick. She had a great houseshare there and we lived the life over that way for a while with her and all her professional mates from their five-bedroomed house on weekends.

Occasionally, we did walk the Ayresome Green tightrope walk on a matchday, and I want to share one last scene with you for your montage. The street was packed with people, a throng you could say, with loads of mounted police towering over them and trying to keep order. I watched this one policeman reach down into the crowd and his hand came up with a little kid, about five, looking like an urchin, twisting and wriggling in his hand. The policeman held him up by the scruff of the neck and bellowed to the crowd, "Does anyone know who this little bloke belongs to?" There was an answer shouted back from a guy in the crowd.

"Yeah, he's mine. But you can keep him!"

"He's too lippy. You have him back!" shouted the copper.

I'll never forget that. It was like street theatre, and we were touching distance.

Like all students away from home in those days, I had an umbilical cord I pulled once a week: the red phone box on the corner of the road, like the one I'd had to phone home sick from at the end of my first term. That's right, children, when you were away from home in those days, you really were on your own. No mobile phones. No social media. No messaging apps. I'd save my coins up in the week. Then, Tuesday night at seven o'clock, I'd be in the queue on the street corner with the other students, jingling their own handfuls of coins, as we waited for the red phone box to be free. You got to know the people who were on the same 'phone home' weekly schedule as you.

I couldn't tell my dad the stories of what happened, some of which I've shared in these pages, because Dad would say, "I told you so! You're not staying up there!" This is the time in your life when you find yourself leaving out significant portions of your life story, as it's not for your parents to share anymore. Which is sad in a way as I loved them dearly and you want your loved ones to know what your life is about. I did let slip some stories to Mum, but on reflection that probably left her worrying. I was religious about phoning them every Tuesday for the same reason, though; Mum would have been worried sick if they didn't hear from me.

Right, no room here for anymore scrapes and adventures from my student years (though there were many more; just ask if you know me and I'll share them). There is, actually, one more scrape to come from within the world of my academic and placement work, ironically, which isn't where you'd expect danger to come from. Before that, I do quickly need to share that I did contribute to college life with activities that weren't all about having fun. I became secretary for the Public Administration Society for the University, for example. I don't do anything by halves, as you know. I said, right, I'm going to invite Tony Benn (the famous Labour MP and sometime Minister for Technology who gave up his peerage and double barrelled surname) to come and speak. The rest of the society said "You don't stand a chance. We've tried inviting everyone of note in the past. They don't come up here to Middlesbrough." It seems to be hardwired in me that if someone says something I would like to do is impossible I tilt at it, Don Quixote-style. So I wrote him a lovely letter inviting him, and he accepted! Tony Benn, the famous radical politician whose firebrand speeches were legendary and inspirational, was coming in response to a letter from little old me. Until ... three days before he was due, with us all ready to welcome him, I received a nice letter from his assistant saying he was so looking forward to coming but he now couldn't as something rather important had come up, meaning all the MPs had to stay in The Commons to deal with it: The Falklands War had been declared. A pretty good excuse for not being able to come. Hard to beat, in fact.

As well as contributing to the life of the college with societies and the like, I did indeed study. Yes, you did read a few paragraphs back an odd word for a student to admit to – I was 'working' in the front room when Jackie called me to the window. I admit it, I did work at my studies. Work hard, play hard and all that.

Which brings me reluctantly to what you might call my *Me Too* moment.

I was coming back from my first lecture at Birmingham Medical Institute that happened to be in the Midlands, so it was familiar territory to me. I knew every road from Birmingham to Shrewsbury, where we were based. It was a sandwich course, remember, and I spent my third year in Shropshire, in the Health Service, having the best possible induction to all departments in the Service. This time was my learning bedrock in more ways than one. The person who had driven me there and was taking me back was a person of responsibility. In theory. He pulled over in a rough cutting just after the Fox at Enville (dark, unlit, a vast wooded area). For no reason. You think fast when that's happening. I knew instantly I could run through the woods and escape to Kinver if I had to. I knew these roads like the back of my hand. Far better than he did. Which is just as well as it gave me a sense of some territorial advantage, information I could use. It would have been terrifying if I had no idea where I was or how to escape if I had to. My hand moved to the door handle.

I've taught my daughter – as a result of what happened to me - that you have to be prepared for these situations. I got ready to respond firmly and with no nonsense. My heart was racing. My hand tightened on the door handle, ready to spill me out of the car if I had to run for it. He turned to me, leant in, started in with the sweet talk. I cut him off, made it clear I was not interested, what did he think he was doing, we had to get back. Not an easy thing to do, standing up to a predatory authority figure who had the destiny of your future career in his hands, in a vulnerable place like that. I held my breath. He started the car up and drove off.

The rest of that journey was the longest, most awkward forty-five minutes in a car I've ever had. I'll never forget it. I go past that place where he pulled over, in those woods, and I see it still, the car stopped there, the danger I was in; I see the escape route I'd worked out in my head and I'm ready to run again if I have to. These turning point events in your life stay with you, frozen in time and place, don't they.

When we got back, one of my housemates could see something was wrong and I told her what had happened. We went through the scenarios that so many women have had to go through when a man abuses a position of power over you at work: if I say something, who do I say it to? He's technically in control so how does that play out? Is it the end of my career if I speak out?

I remember walking into the offices next morning and he was at his desk and it was just another day for him, as if nothing had happened. I remember thinking "This will be OK. I can get through this. He's going to pretend nothing happened and that's the end of it." The relationship from then on was cordial at best, cool for the most part. Until he did it again.

But not to me. The student placed there the following year broke down in tears to me and said he'd tried it on. I felt sick, that it obviously wasn't a one-off but rather his pattern of behaviour and I might have prevented it. But she insisted nothing had actually happened. She was so traumatised by his advances, though, that I knew we had to speak up. That was my first experience of sexual harassment in the workplace and how damaging it can be to your confidence and your sense of work as a safe space.

It was reported to our tutor and no further students were

placed there. Years later, I met him again. I had just been appointed as a Director of HR in the NHS and was at a large meeting in Wolverhampton. He came in and had the gall to sit by me. You can imagine how I felt as I realised it was him. He actually congratulated me. I was cool, calm and collected – just as you hope you'll be in that kind of situation. I professionally acknowledged him, gathered up my things and moved pointedly to sit elsewhere. I felt he totally understood the circumstances and he was put in a very awkward position. He retired sometime later. All I can hope is that I was instrumental in that decision.

The incident certainly helped me have insight into the need for safety in the workplace and that informed my work for years to come, as well as giving me the insight I needed to prepare my daughter, as I've said, in case she came up against anything like that. So, like any painful thing, it had its value.

On a happier note when it comes to my studies …

I got a First in my dissertation. I know, how good is that! I don't want you to think I'm big-headed or anything so will quickly add that I got a 2:2 overall; absolutely fine as a result, but it was the First that provided the platform for my future career.

I was lucky enough in a way that the mission in my head, that led me into the degree I was doing, was to help the NHS get better at managing itself. This tracked all the way back to me observing from the patient's point of view, right back to as a child. This stuff was in my bones now. I could see the need clearly. A consultant could rise to a position of seniority and decision making as a clinical or medical director with no training but their medical degree.

Surely they needed management training? It was so obvious to me; they were figureheads and decision makers.

But, the more I floated and explained my theory, the more it was pooh-poohed. By the consultants themselves – though some of them were less insistent that they already knew it all – but even more surprisingly, the junior doctors I spoke with were more convinced they didn't need it. "Anyone can manage," seemed to be their view.

Cue the re-emergence of stubborn Yvonne. I mean, sometimes in your life you have insights that you just know are right, that might define the future of the profession if you can prove it, and you either fight for it or you take an easy path and forget it. You know me well enough from these pages by now to know which path I took.

I created a questionnaire and spoke to doctors at all levels in the NHS, a comprehensive piece of research if I say so myself. Basically, asking them if they felt they needed management training, what it should cover, and then coming to conclusions about what was actually needed versus the perception of what was needed.

I guess you'd say the mission of my career emerged from that work. If these people were ending up on interview panels, how could you argue that they didn't need training in recruitment and other areas of people management? I had some battles on that over the years to come. If they wanted to sit on disciplinary hearings, as another example, they would need to do the training to get that right, just as the managers on the panel had. All this was to come and, if I've left my mark on the NHS, that's one of the areas where I did it, forging that new discipline of management development for doctors that I'd championed from being a student.

My dissertation was titled *"Do Medical Staff Require Management Training?"*

Did it cause a stir? Well, you could say that, as my work was referenced in the Health and Social Services Journal at the tender age of 21. It became the foundation of my career. The article ended with, "Trainers take note, if ever there was an opportunity of taking an initiative and influencing future patterns of decision making in the service - this is surely it."

Which sets us up for our next adventure – My Brilliant Career. I'm not showing off, it's a pun on the name of a book and film. Keep up. I did do quite well, though. I hope I did important work that helped the NHS, as that was my ambition all along. We'll find out if I succeeded in the next chapters.

Yvonne in her Uni residence

Yvonne in the Uni kitchen, preparing to party

Yvonne eating her carbs
to combat her hangover

Mo and Yvonne at Uni

Yvonne's secret Diary

CHAPTER 5

LIFE IN THE NHS

T racks of my NHS Career

Well, so many to choose from, as my career spanned two decades. But I'll intrigue you by choosing one moment in musical time: blues, salsa and jazz, spilling out into the star- studded night, from the doors and windows of speakeasies and bars to mingle with the breeze whispering through the palm trees around the music district of Old Havana, Cuba. You'll have to wait till the end of this chapter to find out what that's all about. But, to start, what about *Like A Virgin*, by Madonna, to mark my arrival as an innocent first-time manager in the NHS …

First day

Well, I called it, tongue in cheek, my glorious career at the end of the previous chapter. But the first day didn't exactly go to plan. I was due to start my first job – Unit Personnel Manager for a group of hospitals centred around Kidderminster – which is where I would end up working from 1984-7. There was I the night before, looking forward to my Big Day, the first day of my new career that I'd argued with my dad over and studied and worked hard for over the previous few years. Everything led up to this.

The girl from Dudley had big plans, big changes and improvements to make to the NHS that had looked after her over the years and that she wanted to give back to. I'd invested so much in this single-minded goal and had developed a mission, articulated in my dissertation, which was my manifesto of intent – to bring sound management development to the NHS, to make it better.

So, what did I do with all that excitement, all those pre- match nerves? I had a hypo the night before is what I did. I was raring to go in on my first morning, despite needing to recover from the hypo, but my parents put their foot down and my dad called me in sick. On my first day. I was mortified. What a start!

You know me by now, always finding the silver lining. And there was one in the way I stumbled into the first days of my career. My boss, turned out to be a gem. He was completely understanding, made it clear this wasn't a false start, just a one-day postponement and nothing had changed. He could have seen me as a liability. He didn't. He was the unit manager, in fact head of the group of hospitals, and I reported directly to him, so I was going in at quite a high level (personnel manager – no 'HR' in those days).

I went in the next day feeling I'd let them down, but apart from two managers who maybe had a grudge against me (we won't go there) it was the best possible start and I was welcomed with open arms.

I loved my career in the NHS. It was brilliant. It was hard. My career experiences were unbelievable, often joyous, occasionally sad, but the people I worked with were mainly wonderful. I was to go onto some real achievements: I was to rise to Executive Director-level, negotiated wages with over 20 professional and ancillary bodies, worked with all the national unions, staff and patients, won awards, loved it, and hopefully I made a difference.

This was serious work: I was a woman on the first days of a career-long mission that would take decades. But I know what you really want to read about, dear reader: the leg in the laundry, the bomb scare & the biscuit tin, and the time I told the Finance Director to 'Eff Off'. So, we'll start with those, then.

The leg in the laundry

Every Monday morning in my first job, we had a unit management meeting where we agreed what was happening that week. I'd been in post about three weeks when, in the middle of a planning meeting, the Unit General Manager's phone went off. He glanced at it. "I have to take this," he said. Then he went ashen. "We have to end the meeting. I've been called to an emergency," he said, getting up. He turned to me,

"You're coming too. Come on! We've got to get to the laundry." He ran out of the meeting, with me in tow.

The laundry?

We had on our site the laundry for the whole of Bromsgrove and Worcester's hospitals. The way a large industrial laundry works is the bags travel around on overhead pulleys and are then emptied onto conveyor belts to be sorted for the machines. So, this one guy is on his first day as a laundry assistant. He reaches up to a bag above his head that has been routed to him, pulls the drawstring to empty the contents onto his conveyor and … out drops a human leg.

It lands on the conveyor belt, right in front of him. He jumps back in horror, then promptly keels over with a heart attack. The line is stopped and an emergency ambulance is called (to our own laundry).

So, this was my first crisis, my baptism of fire. No amount of scenario planning could have come up with it.

Now, obviously the leg had been amputated in an operation and was on its way to clinical waste. No, not hopping there on its own; in one of those bright yellow clinical waste bags. But the bag had split and the contents had been bundled into a laundry bag by mistake. They're colour-coded, so it shouldn't have happened, but it did. Meaning the leg was diverted from its true destination, the incinerator and, now disguised as harmless laundry, headed instead for its fatal encounter with our new laundry assistant. OK, not quite fatal for him, but it was for his career in the laundry. And I thought my first day had been bad!

When we got there, it turned out the guy was fine, recovering in hospital. But he never came back to work. The possibility of body parts falling out of the sky was just something he couldn't face again. He probably crossed the road for the rest of his life to avoid walking past laundrettes.

My boss was brilliant, advising me what I had to sort out while he went back up the chain of events with the hospital where the bag had come from, doing root cause analysis into how it had happened and what we needed to do to make sure it could never happen again.

I needed to arrange clear and better signage upstream, so to speak, design and implement more and improved induction for the staff, all of which came under my responsibility for training.

The staff in the laundry also needed immediate support, so we brought occupational health in to provide counselling. We also asked the frontline staff what they would advise us to share with the general hospital to make sure it didn't happen again.

I can't remember if that last bit came from me – asking the people on the frontline for process improvement suggestions – but it became a pillar of how I operated from then on, and led to some real changes I made later as 'firsts' in the health service.

147

Such as getting trade union reps and patient representatives onto executive board meetings, which I fought for and won much later in my career.

So, that falling leg in a laundry was an early opportunity for me to get staff input on improvement, a constant tool in my manager's toolbox – and one that the NHS didn't commonly bother wielding, despite its power - a constant in my career that would, decades later, change how NHS boards of directors took in intelligence about what was going on in their organisations from the people on the spot.

In Systems Thinking, which the NHS has been trying to bring in over the past couple of decades, this idea of ensuring the decisionmakers in a board room are in close touch with what is actually happening out in the wards (and the laundries), with frontline staff empowered to give input, is central to improvement. I like to think I championed that from Day One of my career – involving staff at all levels was key to how I approached personnel services. It instinctively felt the right thing to do.

Little Yvonne, back on her diabetic ward, aged nine, was where this came from. She was watchful, she learnt, and she didn't forget. When I was on that ward as a child, I noticed that the domestics were the ones that found out the most information. "How are you today, Yvonne?" they'd say. And I'd go, "Oh, I feel absolutely awful." All the information that I wouldn't tell the staff nurse or the sister, I'd tell the domestic.

Later in my career, we encouraged ward sisters to add the domestics to their team meetings. I said they'll tell you how clean things really are, where the problems are, what the patients are saying to them. They're part of the team, with essential intelligence that you don't hear otherwise.

'One Team' the NHS like to call it now. But I don't see it working as well, as all the common spaces where staff mixed – the canteens, even the smoking rooms, would you believe (all the doctors and nurses smoked!), the grounds that were maintained for staff who lived in, the nurses' quarters, all the staff areas where people of all levels gathered together, shared information and bonded, they're all gone. Cost savings and value for money or a real organisational and patient loss? The glue that holds organisations together is often invisible, doesn't appear in structure charts and in cost-cutting measures.

The bomb scare and the biscuit tin

In among the serious work, I managed the diabetes, and this led to the occasional burst of comedy. Here's one: much later in my career, as a personnel director, I took a call. There might be a bomb in the hospital, said the voice on the other end. It was the days when you'd get bomb hoaxes. But you didn't know if they were a hoax until after, of course. I was one of the most senior people, there with the Deputy Director of Nursing. It was early evening and we had to manage the process of evacuating the danger area until we got the Chief Exec and all the other directors in.

In those days you convened the senior people in a kind of war room of all the managers, with people and information flying in and out of the room to keep on top of evacuating the hospital, liaising with The Bomb Squad, police , fire services and so on. Situations rooms they call them now. So, we're in the middle of this, when I suddenly realise it's 7pm and I haven't eaten.

I ran out of the room, ran down the corridor to my office to grab something essential from my room, and then ran back down the corridor with ... a tin of biscuits. Don't scoff (though I was about to); these were emergency biscuits.

I ran back in and slammed the biscuit tin down on the table. All eyes turned. I realised how odd it seemed to carry into such a high stakes meeting, with such a sense of apparent relief, a biscuit tin. I grabbed a handful to scoff to prevent my blood sugars diving, then offered the tin to the person next to me. "Have a biscuit," I said. "And pass them around." I still felt the need to cover up (as I so often did), by looking like I'd just run out and back for everyone to have a biscuit! The bomb scare was thankfully a hoax, but we only found out after senior managers were walking every floor with the Porters to try and identify anything that might be a suspicious looking package - the bomb! How difficult is that in a busy Specialist Hospital with bits of equipment and packages all over! The Porters and Ward Sisters were our stars that night, helping get all the evacuation measures in place, largely behind the scenes ready for "all systems go". When the police alerted us that it was a hoax, we all stood down, barely minutes from a full evacuation. The Chief Exec took us all to the Hospital Social Club and we shared learning from everyone at every staff level: that is what team working is all about; recognition of the contribution every single role has to play, and the relationships between the roles. I miss that; the NHS is its wonderful staff.

Telling the Finance Director where to go

Right, this one is not one of my finest moments, I have to say in advance. I was prepping a witness in my office for a big case I was leading in London. Later that pm was to be our annual budget and cost improvement setting meeting with all Board members (always stressful for all concerned: I tell you this as this must have been subconsciously playing on my mind to contribute to what happened).

The witness I was preparing for the Case began to suspect something was not right with me. They went out of my office to the Chief Exec's PA and said, "H, I am worried; Yvonne is not right". She popped her head around the door, took one look at me and immediately got on the phone to our Medical Director, whom she knew was in the hospital next door. Bless him, he hotfooted over, dextrose bags in hand, having correctly assumed that Yvonne was going into a Hypo. Just as he charged into our corridor, our Nursing Director arrived to save the day, too. Talk about top level responsiveness to a medical emergency!

As if two Directors weren't enough, the Finance Director, whose office was opposite, stuck her head out to see what was going on. If she'd seen Rocky, the scenes where he's in the corner of the ring, looking out for the count, his medical people working on him, brow being mopped, dextrose syrup being poured into his mouth for energy, she'd have known to back off, not venture forward.

She saw the Medical Director feeding me on one side of my chair whilst the Nursing Director was holding my hand and stroking my brow on the other side. Understandably, she asked if everything was alright. "Obviously not," might have been the politest answer. Instead, she got both barrels. "Fuck off !" I shouted. With great venom, apparently. And she did, sharpish. Wise woman. I wasn't aware of it at the time, but rumour had it afterwards that the two Directors caring for me on either side of my chair were struggling not to collapse laughing while bringing me back to the land of the living. To say the story got around is an understatement: it was told at my leaving party by the Chairman, who said that in all his years he had never had anyone tell the FD to F Off (although thousands would love to) and get away with it.

Remember, I later had to go into the Board-level meeting and fight my corner for funding. And who was it I'd told to F off ? The FD in charge of the purse strings. Did I secure more funding? Did Rocky triumph at the end of that movie? I'm a similarly loveable but unstoppable fighter you know, so I'll leave you to work it out.

On another occasion, also later in my career, my diabetes knowledge came in useful. We were negotiating pay awards with all the staff side reps. There was myself and the chief exec and we were getting to a critical point but one of the reps was going off on one. I knew she was a Type 2 diabetic. And I was feeling a bit low on the blood sugars, so I guessed she was experiencing the same.

I tapped the CEO, on the shoulder and whispered that we need a break. "Is she alright?" she whispered back. "No, I think she's starting to go into a hypo," I replied. "We're going to have a break for a coffee," said CEO. They all looked up because they knew that we didn't do that. Mo came up to me in the break. I said, "You all right?" "No, I need something," she said – language all diabetics instantly understand. I gave her a cup of tea with sugar; she instantly started to feel better, the meeting reconvened and we reached agreement where we might not have done. That was a brilliant moment for both sides.

There was the odd person over the years who might try to undermine you. I had a boss in the NHS who had the infuriating habit, when we were disagreeing on something, of saying, "You alright, Yvonne? Your blood sugar isn't low, is it?" As if the strength of my disagreement was not valid. We had a good relationship, and respected each other; he was a good guy, so I'd generally laugh it off, but you have to be resilient not to let comments like that undermine you. On reflection, you could say the diabetes actually spurred me on, to prove myself against assumptions like that, by trying harder, being more focused and determined. In which case, it helped me achieve to a high level.

I worked my way up to become an Executive Director in the NHS. Of course, you don't achieve anything alone. The people around you inspire you. Particular inspiration and influence, for me, came from my Chief Executive in my last post, Trade Union and Professional Organisation reps over the years and, most of all, the staff. I went into the NHS to help and make change – improving change – and the most satisfaction I got over the years, from day one, was in making changes, from the tiniest improvement to the largest.

Some of the cases where I achieved a change that I'm proudest of were where people would have been discriminated against because the discrimination wasn't being challenged. Someone needed to raise a hand and say this is wrong. Because I knew first-hand the risk of becoming marginalised or even discriminated against – in my case, for medical reasons – that gave me an insight into other people who fell outside 'the norm', and a lot of the changes and even the fights I got into were about standing up for other marginalised people, righting wrongs and trying to make a difference.

I'm not making myself out to be a Nelson Mandela, just to say we can all make this kind of difference if we have a strong sense of what's right and wrong and a determination not to go the easy route, but to do the right thing. We've all seen an example of that recently with the TV drama highlighting the Post Office v Mr Bates scandal (little aside: my nephew was a cameraman on that series). For example, from my own career: We had a student nurse apply to a unit where I was Unit Personnel Officer. The nursing director dismissed the application out of hand, saying, "We can't have her." So, her decision was final. Unless another director argued the case and convinced her otherwise.

The issue with the nurse was that she was missing a forearm, which the nursing director thought disqualified her for the job. One of the clinical tutors came to me and said, "Yvonne, this is unfair. She can do everything the other student nurses can. It may be unconventional, but surely we've got to give her the chance."

What would you do, dear reader? I'm hoping the same as me: I could pitch in on behalf of the nurse and give reasons why she should be given a chance. It was also my role to stand up for people if they were being discriminated against, and to bring in changes to prevent it happening. I took that seriously. I fought the case with the nursing director and won her around. She agreed, the young woman completed her nurse training and then became a brilliant, qualified nurse.

Looking back, the things I am proudest of were like that story about the disabled nurse: helping others achieve against the odds - sometimes evening up the odds by removing barriers for them or fighting for their right to achieve – and standing up for what's right.

I championed a secretary to become a future Director, for example. We all need mentors and champions and it is the most satisfying thing when you see capability in someone, perhaps the system doesn't see it, or the person doesn't see it themselves even, but you clear a path for them or at least encourage them onto the path and help with the support they need to be resilient and keep going.

Fairness has always been so important to me. So, when it came to my attention that our Head of Works (which included responsibility for electrical work), who was a few months shy of his retirement, was about to lose his pension, I did what you'd expect – went in and fought for him. He'd had an eye test, literally months before he was due to retire, and it turned up something he'd never known. And neither had we, his employers. He was colour blind.

Now, electricity wires are colour coded. I know this from my son, who is an electrician. And here we had a guy who had been wiring up and repairing all sorts of hospital electrical equipment, running wiring through buildings and the like, who couldn't tell what colour was what. It turned out, in fact, that he *could* tell which was which, from the shades he saw. He told us this when we asked him how he had managed when he was doing or overseeing hands-on work. No errors had ever been recorded during his career.

He was due to be dismissed early and would lose his pension. Through no fault of his own. He retired on a full pension. And we rechecked all the work he had done over the years to make sure it was safe. Plus, we implemented additional checks and balances. Your job, at least in part, as a Unit Personnel Officer, is to support your staff; not just enforce personnel policies, with people feeling 'done to' by HR, but to fight their corner. That's how I always saw it, anyway. And you needed that attitude – a readiness to make a stand when you saw something unfair, maybe the 'bloody mindedness' my dad recognised in young Yvonne – if you were to make a difference.

And, that was my personal mission, always: to make a difference. It got me into fights, of course. I led a long fight through the courts in London to get a senior manager struck off for patient abuse. And won. On a larger, institutional, scale, I helped close an old asylum and replace it with a wonderful new, acute Mental

Health hospital, which I'm so proud to have been a part of.

My NHS career gave me achievements and experiences I never dreamed I would encounter. It gave me a purpose and the realisation that you can achieve if you put your mind to it, and you can make change happen, however big or small. You can make a real difference.

A word on being a woman in the NHS. Yes, there are plenty of female senior managers now. There certainly weren't when I started. The number of senior level meetings I attended where the only woman was the HR person (personnel, remember?) and, yep, that was me, were countless. You had to hold your own. And not be phased by being the odd one out. Again, you could say the diabetes helped me with that, as the odd one out was my default setting internally, at least in terms of my self-perception.

Understanding the importance of diversity – of how (dis)ability, ethnicity, gender, age and so on can exclude people from decision-making positions of responsibility in a workplace culture, however unconsciously – means taking steps to listen intently to the experiences of others, to immerse yourself in their experience if you can. That need to understand took me to a diversity meeting for women at the NEC. Before the event, one or two of my staff asked if I should go, as the meeting wasn't 'for' me; it was for women of colour in the NHS to discuss common issues they were facing. "I need to understand how women from all different origins and backgrounds feel in the NHS workplace, that's part of my portfolio," I said. "So, yes, I need to be there." Unfortunately, I arrived ten minutes late due to unforeseen hold ups on the way. I was indeed one of only a few women in that room, as far as I can remember, who was not visibly from a diverse When I walked into the already-packed auditorium, my colleagues were so brilliantly welcoming, standing up so I could see them and waving me over into a seat. I learnt so much that day, with the help of my colleagues, and hope that we continued to improve the sense of belonging and welcome that all our multi-diverse colleagues felt working in the organisation we were all employed in, just as I was made to feel included and welcomed at that meeting. With any kind of exclusion, you have to reach a stage where it is just no longer an issue; whatever level meeting you walk into in the NHS or whichever employer, it should not be notable that there is a mix of gender, ethnicity, (dis)ability and age among the decision-makers in the room; it should just be the norm. From when I entered the NHS to when I left, and it was always a priority of mine, so I do hope I helped.

You had to make small stands yourself in those days, though, where almost all senior NHS managers and consultants you worked with were male. If your natural inclination and even role in life is to care, as it is for most women (more on my role as a carer for family and friends in a later chapter, but we all do it) then you have to learn to ration that in the kind of work I did, at the kind of level I was at. Let me explain with an example:

I'll never forget a late evening meeting in Sandwell, where I was the only female, being told by a Senior Consultant how he liked his tea whilst I was pouring out mine before going to sit down. I held back my natural inclinations and replied, "I'll be out of your way in a moment," and left him to get his own. The expectation was that I would make his. If we'd been female managers together, that's the kind of thing women do for each other without a thought; it's not an issue. It becomes an issue when a 'senior' male asks a 'senior' female to make his tea, even if it's not done consciously. Would he have said the same to a senior male colleague? Definitely not. It certainly wasn't like that when I left the NHS but it meant enough back then for me to mention it to Tony when I got home as a "cheeky sod" kind of story.

There are times, thankfully, when you don't have to have your guard partly up. It may be no coincidence that my chief exec was phenomenal. And we worked hand in hand together. We were the first trust to have a female chief exec, a female finance director and a female director of HR. And we bought a different personality and way of doing things to the board, I've no doubt about that.

That was where I introduced patient and staff representation on executive boards. I had a phenomenal relationship although I say it myself, with the trade unions and the professional organisations and we got so many things done as a result. Can you imagine how much more trusting the relationship is when the TU reps – and patient reps (wow, what a fight I had to get that to happen) – are privy to the finance meetings that explain the financial restraints, so know exactly what the situation is, rather than those meetings happening behind closed doors.

Here's one example of what we achieved by reaching decisions together like this: I was invited to Belfast to address a conference as the keynote speaker and tell other NHS Trusts how we'd achieved something that hadn't been done before. The Conference was hosted by the BBC's Sophie Raworth. As an aside, she gave me a public apology for having to reduce my presentation time because previous speakers had run over. I had to adapt the talk with five minutes' warning to the shortened time! I asked to have a roaming mike, instead of a lectern, and paced the stage in front of all the NHS Health Directors, including Wales, England, NI and Scotland. I did it, my staff signing to me how many minutes I'd got left, so I hit the timing spot on. Boy, I needed that G & T after, and boy I reckon Sophie's ears were burning .

The award I and my colleagues from Primary Care received was for the creation of the first strategic workforce and training plan that brought all of the organisations providing mental health services together.

As I said in the talk, when you mapped out the touch points with those organisations for a person with mental health issues, the number of people knocking on their door and walking over their threshold from the different agencies was mind-blowing. There was so much duplication that you could have 20 people going into their homes when you could have achieved the same outcome with, say, five. The resource that is then freed up could be redirected, maybe towards unmet need – those who never got a visit - and for other developments in mental health. Not the kind of thing you see splashed across tabloid headlines, but the effect of our change was ground-breaking.

Coming runner up at the Excellence in HRM Awards 2006 for HR Director of the Year was another high point.

Time to end this whistle stop tour of my NHS career, which we started with a false start on the first day and an amputated leg in a laundry in the third week, you may remember, only to end up decades later, in an unlikely enchanting place that I will never forget: Cuba.

Surprised you there, didn't I? As I progressed from unit to unit, hospital to hospital within the Midlands, you weren't expecting us to end up on a tropical island off the coast of Florida.

Cuba has a remarkably well-developed health service, you might like to know. They have the highest number of doctors per head of population in the world, above super-rich countries Monaco and Switzerland, that trail in second and third. Remember the early days of Covid, when Italy was particularly overwhelmed in Europe and needed more doctors? Perhaps you don't, but the doctors they needed were sent by Cuba. Despite the decades of economic embargoes they have lived with.

So, spending two weeks in Cuba, learning from their health service and helping them by sharing innovations and systems that worked for us is where my Chief Executive and I ended up. Hence the love of blues, salsa and jazz that I now have today and that opened this chapter.

It was a magical two weeks. Hard work in the day, but enormous fun sampling the nightlife, sitting down the front with a Cuba Libra at a small table in a packed nightclub, as The Buena Vista Social Club or some other wonderful local band had you swaying until it was uncontrollable and you had to get up and join the locals in dancing the night away.

The one downside? My partner in crime (and boss) our CEO, with whom I should have been bonding over the Cuba Libres, was not a great fan of the smoke-filled music cellar bars. Deep sigh. Well, no-one's perfect. But my, how she turned heads when she walked through the streets of Havana, celebrity-like, with ice white cropped hair.

So, we have to leave Yvonne, salsa-ing into the night in Old Havana, cigar in one hand, rum in the other, handsome gigolo giving her the eye from across the dancefloor (I'm exaggerating! There was no cigar …) and wind the clock back in our story. Because there's a whole load of husband- meeting, romance, weddings (well, one wedding) and children going on while all the above NHS career was happening. Us girls multitask. Read on, then, for the other dimensions of our story that were running parallel to my NHS life: tales of love, and caring, of more challenges thrown up (and largely overcome) by diabetes, the joy of creating new life, a new generation, and the bitter-sweet sadness of looking after and then saying goodbye to the previous one.

Yvonne & her CEO in Cuba

Mental Health history in Cuba

Cuba Libra! Dancing in the…

CHAPTER 6:

LOVE AND FAMILY

Tracks of these years

Let's stick with just one for now: Gold (Spandau Ballet). Why? Because in 1985 I met the love of my life and my better half, Tony, who is pure gold. Chance encounters, eh? We stumble into our life's greatest love affair, Sliding Doors-style (you know; that movie about how a tiny random event can shape your future happiness). If we'd gone the other way or, in my case, not gone into a house when I dropped a friend off, we'd never have met. And I wouldn't have made her homeless. I'm getting ahead of myself again, dear reader. Settle down and I'll explain.

Meeting Tony

I was studying for my professional qualifications at Wolverhampton Uni, along with a friend, Julie, whom I used to drop off at home each week. One night she invited me in for coffee. I walked in through the front door. And the course of my life shifted. Did you feel an earth tremor in 1985 wherever you were? The ground shift just a bit beneath your feet? It was that momentous a meeting, it would turn out, that I wouldn't be at all surprised at the seismic consequences. You wouldn't have guessed it at the start, though, when Julie and I walked into the front room to see two blokes watching TV: her landlord and his best mate.

That was Tony and his perennial friend Steve. We joined them, had coffee and a chat. Was it love at first sight? I don't know. But a seed was planted with those coffee beans because, a few weeks later, Tony rang and asked me to go for a drink. Now, it could have all fallen apart at this point; those sliding doors were in danger of clanging shut at the wrong moment, sending each of us spiralling off in the wrong direction, into different lives. I shudder to think.

I couldn't go out on the date he asked for as I was seeing work colleagues that evening, I explained. He persisted (thankfully), ringing back and suggesting another date. When I heard his voice on the 'phone I was so happy that he'd tried again. So, all set to start the romance of the century, right? Not quite. On the day of the date, I had a rotten cold. I had to call him and say, through sneezes and sniffles down the phone, that I was not going to make it as feeling unwell. He said, calmly, not to worry, that he understood of course, and I should look after myself. But I know his patience was being tested. Was this woman he clearly liked mucking him about? He gave me one more chance. Thank the stars, else we might not be here today - and our wonderful kids! On such small decisions do our lives and those of future generations turn.

Finally, that first date happened. We went to The Cat at Enville. My Tony (as he was to become) doesn't drink. I had a pint. He had an orange juice. Picture that scenario for a sec: a couple at a pub, sitting opposite each other, the petite woman with the pint, the tall handsome fella with the orange juice. Heads leaning in towards each other. Slightly oblivious of everyone and everything else around them. Because that became the motif of our nights out together as a couple for thirty-plus years. Me and my man.

It was maybe our fourth date when Tony announced that he wanted to take me to London, to see the band Supertramp, at the Albert Hall no less. This was a step up from a drink down the local! We both worked fulltime, and the gig was in the week, so we had to be there and back in the one evening. I was still living at home, remember, under the strictures of very watchful, loving parents who now had me back under their roof and therefore felt they had a say (Dad, that is) in what was not a good idea for his Yvonne. London and back in one night was slightly bonkers in his view. They didn't want me to go. But I wasn't to be swayed from my adventurous big date in London. Only, it turned out to be a threesome.

Tony pulls up onto our drive, jumps out to get me
… and out jumps his mate Steve from the passenger
side door, too. So, not the romantic twosome trip to
London I'd been expecting then! But the budding
romance survived. Far from derailing the love affair by
being the proverbial third wheel, Steve became a great
friend to the two of us.

I moved into Tony's house, after giving notice to
his two female tenants, one of whom, Julie, was the
reason I met Tony in the first place. Sorry, Julie, but
love comes first. I'm sure she understands. Though she
might have regretted asking me in for coffee right at
the start as she later perused the 'rooms to let' ads.

One of the earliest tests of our relationship came
when Tony's mum went to Canada to visit his brother
Peter. We decided to surprise her by redecorating her
lounge while she was away. Both of us working 10
hours a day, decorating at night, what on earth could
go wrong? Tempers frayed, the bonds between us were
tested, it all could have ended there and then. But these
testing ordeals, when you're both up against it and
performing tired and under pressure, can either forge
bonds or break them, can't they. You see what each
other's like under duress. And you learn to embrace
that. Nanny Irene's face was a picture on her return.
I'll never forget it

I must have proved myself. Because not long after
the lounge makeover challenge, Tone took me to the
Anchor in Kinver, a top-class establishment in those

days, (I remember every item of clothing I wore that evening) and he proposed. Well, you know what my answer was. We went home, he spoke to Dad and Mum, as you did in those days. There were no objections from them. I remember hugs and beaming smiles all round. Mum even had a sherry (love you so much, Mum).

Wedding day

We were married on the 19 September 1987. It was the best day of my life. The catalogue of things that went wrong, as you are about to read, just added to how memorable it all was. Looking back, it was a glimpse of things to come as our future married life was to be just as eventful.

We were married at St Benedict's, Wombourne, with a reception in Wolverhampton. Mum, Dad, Graham, Jack (Graham's lovely wife) and I stayed at the hotel the night before. We had a meal together and I was about to go up to my little room. It was fine, but it was a single, whereas Graham and Jackle's was a lovely old stone walled double. Looking around my plain little room, it didn't feel like the special night-before-your-wedding place I'd hoped for. I was sad and wished I was home. There was a knock at the door. "Pack up, you are moving room," declared my amazing brother. He gave up their room for the bride to be and I moved in with Jackie, who had even prepared the en suite luxury bath for me, so I felt totally pampered.

171

The next morning, we were downstairs at breakfast when Mum suddenly pushed me under the table. She had seen Tony and Steve roll up to drop off the cars. It was bad luck for us to see each other, so she kept me down there, under the table. Tony took his time and I was on the floor under the table throughout. Mum and I laughed when he'd gone and she let me back up again. What a near miss, we thought, and went up to get ready. And that's when the electricity cut out.

I couldn't do my hair and the staff were worrying about how they'd prepare the wedding breakfast and host all the guests with no power. Jackie, my ace sis-in-law, kept me calm until all the lights came back on. Oh, my wonderful electrician son, how we could have done with you shooting back in time and riding to the rescue then.

We managed to get the bride (me) ready for her big moment. As we walked down the stairs a couple from America made me feel very special, oohing and aahing and asking for a photo. Can't have scrubbed up that badly, then, despite the power cut.

I got into the car in all my ivory gown finery with Dad, who promptly offered me a Mars Bar. "You need to keep your sugars up," he declared. "I can't get chocolate on my wedding dress," I countered, aghast and we had a row in the car. Typical! Dad had filled his pockets with emergency Mars Bars. What a star.

Our honeymoon plan was Dubrovnik. But it was bombed the week before, part of the civil war that led to the splitting up of the former Yugoslavia. It's still on my bucket list, so maybe we'll get there for a second honeymoon sometime soon (hint, hint to one particular reader). So, we rescheduled and headed for Ibiza, dropped at the airport this end by Best Man Steve.

Ibiza, glamorous clubbing destination, the trendiest and most stylish of all the Ibearic islands. You can imagine how we thought our honeymoon would be. Pretty swanky. The second day we came down with food poisoning. Tony had his first real introduction to living with Diabetes (imagine trying to keep your blood sugar levels right while going through a bout of food poisoning). You could say he met my diabetes face to face for the first time. And proved himself up to it. He passed with flying colours, despite being as ill as I was with the food poisoning. We had each other and we had a lovely honeymoon. It was all-action: I won a shooting competition, Tony was hauled out of the pool and sidelined for ducking a competitor in a water polo tournament, only to redeem himself by being the star in an orchestral body performance. He had to go up on stage and have his body bent into instrument shapes and then 'played' by the on-stage performers. He was bent into the shape of a cello – without his flexibility and athleticism it wouldn't have worked – and 'played' by a beautiful musician actress. Of course I wasn't jealous!

We returned home, relieved to have had a wonderful wedding and honeymoon despite all the setbacks and unexpected events, when Steve dropped another bombshell. He picked us up from Gatwick. As he walked us up to the car, he was in full-blown apology mode, confessing to how Tone's much-loved Escort Sport had been banged up in an accident. What an end to our honeymoon! Tony's face was ashen when he saw the car in the distance as we approached it, all battered and dented. Until he got close and the damage didn't look quite right. Tony peered closer still. Then burst out laughing when he realised Steve had somehow painstakingly covered the car in fake self-adhesive panels that were beaten up and dented. He got us good with that one.

The marriage hi-jinks weren't quite over. We arrived home to a sheet across the house welcoming the honeymooners back and our bedroom filled with over a hundred balloons. Tone's mum had helped but hadn't realised that half the balloons were inflated Durexes. They looked so odd that she apparently kept saying she thought they were faulty and whoever bought them should get their money back. God bless her. It was a hoot.

Yvonne & Tony's Wedding

Talking of hoots, the end of the 80s also saw the end of my saxophone-playing career. Oh, I didn't mention that? Well, back to the tracks of these years, then, as Gerry Rafferty's Baker Street, with its soaring sax at the heart of the song, is key to this time of my life. Keen readers will remember I've loved the sax since hearing it in my parents' records as a child. And my love of the sax was part of how Tony found his way into my heart.

I told him about how the sound of the saxophone touched my heart. Sometime later, he touched my heart himself, buying me a saxophone as a surprise present. This was not long after we had started "courting". I had lessons (from a great sax player who was in the Black and White Minstrels Orchestra). I could play a basic tune. My future dual career beckoned: daytime HR person, working her way up the NHS ladder, with a night-time alter ego as the Midlands' own homegrown jazz sax diva, propping up the bar at Ronnie Scotts' Birmingham after a successful gig, then having to race home to be ready for work the next morning. Only, fate intervened. In the form of a lost finger. (Trigger warning for the squeamish).

A year after our marriage, my saxophone-playing possible future evaporated. I had a motorbike accident. As a result of which, I eventually lost the little finger on my right hand.

Suffice to say, I've only picked up the saxophone, which I still love, a few times since then (once, memorably, to perform at a party, but that's the next chapter).

Perhaps one day, when I have more time, and someone's invented an artificial finger or aid that will work on the saxophone (the little fingers are important on a sax) I look forward to having another go. It's not currently top of my bucket list, but I still sometimes, when no-one's looking, get my sax, given to me by Tony, out of its case to bask in its beauty and all the memories. Name no names about whose bike came off the back of, but thanks Steve.

It was Steve's quick-thinking and expert bike handling

probably saved us from it being a lot worse. My friend from Uni, Mark (who had, incidentally, been diagnosed with Type 1 Diabetes after finishing his studies), was visiting and we were all going out for the day. I thought it'd be fun to recreate Uni days when I'd regularly ride on the back of a mate's bike. Of course, Dad popped around when I was getting ready and made his disapproval known (he had a bike back in the day, so knew it could be dangerous). Which made it all the more awkward for Tony later in the day when he had to break the news to Dad that I was in an ambulance on the way to hospital. A giant American Cadillac had taken us out, Steve and I. We ended up off the bike, sailing over a wall into someone's front garden, swiftly joined by the bike itself. Tony was travelling with us but in the car, which he promptly leapt out of to confront the Cadillac driver, only to have to be restrained by Mark, which was just as well, as the driver was about seven foot tall and had a couple of angry looking Alsatians in the car with him.

Not long after we were married, we bought our first house together. All we could afford was an absolute wreck, though it was in a lovely location. Turning the wreck you can afford into a home together is a rite of passage for so many couples, as testing as it is. Literally homemaking. Making over Nanny Irene's lounge was a walk in the park by comparison. We had a standpipe in the garden for a while as our water supply. Then we found an unwanted alternative water supply under the kitchen – an ancient well, of all things! We had to fill it in, living those first months all the while with bare brick walls, no carpet on the floors or, looking up, even no ceilings! During which time my brother got a new job in The Lakes and we had sister-in-law move in with us for a few months, whilst they found their family home up north (where we have since spent many a happy adventure).

For Tony's thirtieth birthday we had a Scalextric party at the house. All the lads brought theirs around, joined them together and we had our own Silverstone running all around the house. To mark the special occasion, I spray painted '30' over all the walls in bright scarlet.

A brilliant, unforgettable end to the 1980s. But, the next decade was to be even more momentous on the family front.

The 1990s

What a decade. I had two beautiful babies, Harriet in 1992 and Thomas in 1997. As wonderful as it was to bring these two remarkable people into the world, it wasn't plain sailing. Type 1 diabetes pregnancies can be hard. You are learning to balance your blood sugars while carrying around a separate growing person who is drawing on your supplies, so to speak, as they grow. In 1990, I lost a baby, so our awareness of what could happen at worst was heightened, as you can imagine, when I became pregnant with Harriet just a short year or so after that loss. I still have the letters from my consultant advising me that my diabetic control and health were back to where they needed to be for Tony and I to start trying again.

The care I received was excellent. Every time I went into the hospital on the way to work, for the baby's heart monitoring, I had a bag packed ready in the car, just in case. More than once, the readings led them to be ultra cautious and admit me. They put me in a side room, which partly I didn't like, as I wanted to be in the thick of it, where the open ward was, as I love learning about how the NHS is working on the shop floor, so to speak. But I was also grateful, as I was able to hold work meetings in my little side room. The nursing staff kept sandwiches back for Tony as he'd always turn up after work, five minutes before the end of visiting hours bell went. They passed him his sandwiches and let him stay.

With the staff knowing I was part of the NHS, we had a relaxed lack of formality about how we worked with each other to manage my control. I knew the demands on my Registrar and he knew I understood. So he visited me much later at night when his punishing schedule was quieter and we sat on the corridor floor with a coffee agreeing our diabetes management plan and required insulin levels for the next day. He couldn't have readily done that with the other patients!

I did ask to go on the ward in the later stages of my pregnancy. Seeing the day-to-day operation of the ward gave me a lot of "food for thought" in my hospital planning roles. I was back to little Yvonne observing from her hospital bed in that diabetic ward all those years before, spotting things that could be better. Whenever I go with family and friends to a clinic, I am a nightmare as the first 10 minutes of the journey home is always saying how wonderful our NHS is but … and then I rattle off a list of things that need to improve. They've got used to it. Or they've stopped listening.

Harriet was born by planned C section, taken out of my arms and straight to the Special Care Baby Unit to metabolise for a few days. I wanted to love and hold her, was craving some form of bonding with her. So, we got the nurses to set up a wheelchair and drips to get me safely to the SCBU. Tony had to promise on his own life that he would monitor me and at the slightest sign anything was wrong he would rush me back or would call them. We were with her within a few hours. My bloods were variable, but I had a very precious bundle to care for, so I *had to* make sure I was stable. My tendency is to be outward-caring rather than inward-caring, apparently. Knowing how devastated my parents would be, and Graham, if I got it wrong had always sharpened my focus on the management of my diabetes. With children, Tony, the people at work I had to be fit and competent to help care for and, later, the older generation I was caring for, a loving circularity developed; I had to look after myself to be able to look after them. Never did this need feel so imperative as when I was stood there holding each of my children for the first time, responsible for this wonderful little scrap of life.

I was back to work within ten weeks. Work and personal circumstances needed me, but Harriet had many adventures in her early years in the hospital nursery. She was trouble. A chip off the old block, methinks. It definitely helped that the nursery came under my portfolio at that time. For example, there was the occasion when she was three and with her two friends, one of whom was the Midwifery Director's daughter, they put the plugs in the sinks and turned all the taps on in the nursery bathroom, flooding the place. We'll draw a veil over that one, to save Harriet's blushes. The Three Musketeers, the staff called those three, for all the mischief they got up to.

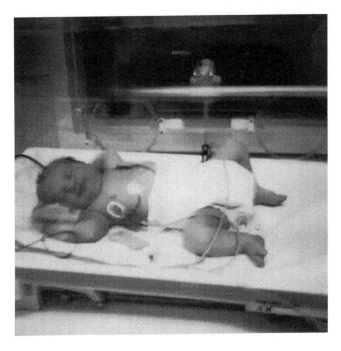

Baby Harriet

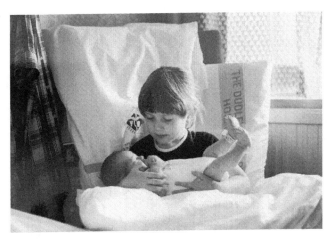

Harriet and Baby Thomas after SCBU

I then moved jobs, became a director and had my second baby in 1997. Pregnancy again was eventful but if you work at it, you manage it and you have the most wonderful gift at the end. Thomas was born with polycystic kidneys. This had been detected before birth and so we knew an operation was inevitable. He was born tiny, beautiful and otherwise fine. There was an unwelcome additional event after the relief and happiness of welcoming him into the world, however. No sooner had I got home with Thomas, than I was whisked away from him to be re-admitted and re-opened up due to infection; a swab had been left in me when he was born! After this second invasive procedure, we were both home safe and we could carry on enjoying the wonder of the new addition to the family. He was so small, though, that we had to wait until 2005, when he was big enough to go through the operation he needed to have a kidney removed. Those eight hours Thomas was being operated on were the longest time imaginable.

My diabetic consultant at the time was also my mum's physician. Can you imagine the complexity of trying to keep your bloods balanced through all of that – childbirth, childcare, career, unexpected health worries for your baby, plus increasing concern for my mum, who was not well. I can't thank him enough for steering me through. Talking of Mum, time to turn to one of the hardest things I had to face, caring for her and then, ultimately, saying goodbye to her. It turned out she was the first of a number of relatives I was to help care for at the end of their life.

My wonderful Mum

Learning to care

After Thomas's birth, Mum started to decline in health. By the time Harriet was six and Thomas was one, I was looking after them, managing a demanding job and had become Mum's main carer with Dad, and Graham travelling down every other weekend (he had two toddlers) until she passed away at 67. I'm so glad she got to see and love her grandchildren, on my side and Graham's. Those years tested my resilience, but she was my life and is still with me now in thought and in my heart, every day. We learn through experience, don't we, and I was learning as I went through that with Mum. A carer in training.

Over the subsequent years, helping the older generation in our family through their last years as well as seeing my kids through their first years became a major part of my life. At any one time I was caring for or helping to care for at least one member of our family. After my mum, Tony's mum started to decline through Alzheimer's. We cared for her at home until it was taken out of our hands. His aunty then developed terminal cancer and my caring turned to her. I was becoming an expert thanks to the privilege of looking after these amazing people in their last years. My dad with dementia and COPD was next, the caring shared with Graham again, and after his passing (during the time of Covid), we now care for my step mum Betty, a formidable woman. Not to mention our Buster, her pet dog, who has been bequeathed to Tony (taking on the canine caring responsibilities).

Love and loss are two sides of the same coin. We express our love for those who have raised us when we turn into their carers in their last years. It doesn't make it any the less painful to say goodbye, but it is some consolation knowing you have been able to show your love with the level of determination and even ferocity that terminal care requires – It needs to be a fierce love to hang in there and keep you focussed on their needs not your sense of loss.

These long and loving farewells are rites of passage and as essential an ongoing act of love as the raising of our children. But, oh, how I look back and wish I'd cared for Mum at the end of that long learning curve of caring instead of right at the beginning. I still had L plates on when I started with Mum. If I'd learnt through those other caring experiences and then finished with Mum she'd have had the ultimate level of daughterly care lavished upon her, with all the things I'd learned about how best to do it.

These times in your life are unforgettable. They stay with you forever. I will just describe one goodbye, and then we'll move on.

It can't be my Mum's, as it still hurts too much today to write about those last days of her care, but I do have a wonderful story to share about Mum, after she had passed, just before I share a story about the last days of care for another family member.

As an astute reader, you'll remember the Bible Cadbury's gave her on getting married? Of course you do. Two months after she passed away, Dad gave that precious Bible to me, after I had just been confirmed in the Church, which was something I had promised Mum I would do. It was a lovely evening. The Bishop of Worcester turned up unexpectedly to join us who were getting confirmed. The Vicar asked me to do the reading (no pressure, then).

Mum would have been so proud. I know she was with me.

And that she was laughing with us at what happened next. It was a very cold, frosty November evening - beautiful - and when we walked back from Church (Tony, Aunty M, Dad, Thomas and Harriet), that was the moment Harriet chose to come out with her first swear word. Blasphemous or what! On such an evening! We were at the front door, freezing, fumbling with the keys and this little voice said, "Hurry up, I'm bloody cold." Time stood still. Grandad swung round and admonished her, but you could tell he was doing his best not to laugh. I got the keys and Tony ushered her inside and up to bed, giving her what for along the way. We all went into the kitchen and cried with laughter, but boy was she in for it tomorrow.

OK, with that loving nod and a smile to Mum, we turn back to describing one of the goodbyes we had to go through with the older generation of our family, the last days of care that are so important as an act of love, as important as the welcoming of the new generation when they come into the world.

Aunty Val had been diagnosed with terminal cancer and we had been caring for her until it was time for her to go into the hospice for the final few days. I had arranged the home support services she needed, accompanied her to appointments and looked after Uncle Arnold. On the day she was going to Mary Stevens Hospice in Stourbridge, I had again stayed the night with them. This was to be Aunty Val's last night in her own home.

The neighbours and family all trooped in, one after the other, to say their goodbyes. It was beautiful and very special. That morning, I got up, did the best to make myself presentable, spoke to Tone, who popped in on his way to work to tell Aunty Val he'd see her later when she was settled into her new place, got Uncle Arnold ready and spent time with Aunty Val. We held hands and looked out on her lovely garden that her neighbour had made beautiful for her, the garden that Harriet and Thomas had played in so happily while Aunty Val and I looked on. Aunty Val held my hand and said, "This is the last time I will see it, isn't it." We looked at each other and I said, "Yes".

The ambulance came. The paramedics were brilliant, navigating the bed out to the front. The neighbours were all out, waving and smiling. I broke down, maybe for the first time in public. They'd never seen me cry and another neighbour, six feet tall, enveloped me in a bear hug, whispered in my ear, "Put your big girl pants on", meaning continue to finish the journey with strength for Aunty Val.The aforesaid neighbour who had been a star throughout, thrust a mountain of tissues into my hand, which I worked through in my car as I followed the ambulance to Aunty Val's hospice. It was as if the heavens were pouring down and through me. I needed windscreen wipers for my eyes and Tony was talking to me all the way to keep me from foundering and sinking. The song Supermarket Flowers by Ed Sheeran was playing in my head:

> "I took the supermarket flowers from the windowsill. I threw the day old tea from the cup ...
>
> Oh I'm in pieces, it's tearing me up, but I know
>
> A heart that's broke is a heart that's been loved."

His words in that song reflected everything I was experiencing. What you learn with diabetes, and also with the loss of those you have loved, when their time comes, is that the awful and the wonderful can happen at the same time, in fact be the same thing. It was an awful episode but a wonderful one, knowing how much Aunty Val was loved and sharing a most precious part of it.

I also had the greatest privilege of preparing her funeral flowers (no supermarket flowers for my family, Ed), as I did for Jackie's mum (my first floristry assignment) and thereafter Tony's mum, my dad and, heartbreakingly, our best friend's grandchild, little Tillie. Every piece of foliage and flower had my heart in them. I feel the floral arranging I have returned to (and trained in), since those long-ago days when little Yvonne presented a jar of pansies to our appreciative neighbour - nestled in a tiny wheelbarrow made from an eggbox - has allowed me a beautiful opportunity to express my personal goodbyes through lovingly-crafted floral tributes.

Right, having brought you along with me in floods of loving tears – I find myself surrounded by tissues again as I write this – we need to stop boosting the profits of the Kleenex company and turn to the need for joy. Yes, there is a bittersweet joy in caring for and saying goodbye to those you love, as aching as it is. But our next chapter looks at how you need to work at joy, my wonderful readers. For my family, joy is getting together with crazily creative parties, full of surprises. So, throw away those tissues, pick yourself up and get your glad rags on. Got your sparkly boa ready? Head held high? Good. Link arms with me and best foot forward. We're going partying.

Yvonne's floral creative designs for a local church charity event, based on musicals

Aunty Val in her beloved garden with the kids

CHAPTER 7:

A TIME TO DANCE

Ah, before we can go partying, there's a small family rebellion to deal with. Family and friends, actually.

They're swarming around me now, saying that I need to give them space in these pages to let you see me and my life from their perspective.

Tony says the people around a person see their life from a different perspective and there are sides to me and living with diabetes that I underplay. He's insisting … Oh, go on then. For the sake of a bit of family peace. Here he comes …

Tony speaks

"Right. The husband needs to have a say here. As you've heard, I met Yvonne when she visited my house to drop off her college course friend as they were both doing their professional exams at the time. She rented a room from me. My friends called me Rigsby, a tragic landlord from a TV series, people of a certain age will remember. I was struck by Yvonne's happy infectious nature. I soon grew to recognise and be won over by her positive attitude to all her life's trials and tribulations.

Yvonne may not know what her dad said to me when I asked for her hand in marriage, so I'll share that here. It was a cold winter's night in January. We'd been out for a meal, during which I had popped the question. Then it was back to hers to ask for her hand. Yvonne took her Mum into the kitchen. This left me with her father, who was my idea of the toughest sergeant major you can imagine. The question I had to ask him came out - with some difficulty. Thankfully, Les gave his blessing but added the caveat that I knew her condition. I said yes, I knew what I was buying into and wouldn't let her down. He could trust me with his daughter. But I couldn't have possibly understood then nor do I know completely now what Yvonne puts up with day in day out.

Very occasionally when at a low ebb, she will say, 'I just want a day off'. Then, within a very short space of time, she'll be back to her fighting best. I imagine it as having a set of weighing scales (like the Old Bailey Court of Justice type) setup in a Type 1 Diabetics body. Countless factors can upset the balance, from the clock changes twice yearly, to stress levels, exercise, to coming down with a cold. Exercise comes with a three-page medical guidance note for diabetics that you have to master before you even don your running shoes. When you have an illness there's another 'Insulin Sick Day Rules' document you have to remind yourself of because being sick changes your insulin needs.

A normal body's pancreas constantly gauges the correct amount of insulin at the correct time 24/7. Yvonne's hasn't worked since age 9. She relies on the Tslim/Dexcom closed loop insulin pump system nowadays, which still requires constant attention for cannula changes, transmitter changes, sensor changes, including 3-day, 10-day and 2-monthly interventions, not to mention daily blood glucose, insulin and carbohydrate counting.

Yvonne relies on pharmacies and drug companies for basic human survival. And she relies on the technology working. Sometimes it doesn't. Inevitably. Imagine if your Dexcom system, which is advising the Tslim pump of the state of your blood glucose, is malfunctioning, which has happened, and it's out of hours and you call them up and listen to the message machine reporting that, "Our offices are now closed. If you need urgent clinical assistance go to A & E" or "Our lines are busy , we will call you back". Your average A & E doctor will not understand the complex workings of the Tslim closed loop system, so Yvonne refers back to her Emergency Back-up, which involves resorting to manual injections whilst sorting the problem. Of course, the crisis generates stress and that in itself impacts Yvonne's body chemistry and has to be factored in. She has to think of everything.

Just over a year ago, Yvonne received an Urgent Field Safety Notice, requiring an update to the pump's software. There was a host of information and Yvonne waited for me to return home to start initiating the update involving technical support over the phone, whilst I manned the laptop and Yvonne updated the pump. It must have taken two hours and then the wait to ensure all was working correctly was tense. Over the next week Yvonne said how much better she was feeling and that she felt the pump was working correctly now. Previously she had been saying "This pump is not all it's cracked up to be". Happy days! Yvonne hates technology but she grapples successfully to keep on top of it, constantly quizzing me, Harriet and Thomas as her 24/7 IT support. Thank goodness she does, as it is her lifesaver.

I understand people have trauma in their lives, but few have it for ALL their life. Yvonne looked at an exciting piece of homemade walnut cake this Christmas made by her sister-in- law, saying "I'd love a piece of that!" But it would likely have sent her blood glucose into orbit, and she didn't want to feel rotten for any part of the family celebrations, so it was a no- no.

Trying to navigate the security section in an airport has been another fun series of encounters for us over the years, more so recently. An insulin pump is not compatible with the scanning equipment these days, so it ends up us requesting a manual search and swab instead of walking through the scanner. This isn't something we have an issue with; it's for all our safety. But it's not always an easy process. I remember one particularly tough experience with a staff member at Schiphol airport in the Netherlands. A little bit of power and a uniform goes to some people's heads. Yvonne had to stand her ground and refuse to go through the scanner, all the time trying to share documentation that explained why she couldn't.

Another quality of Yvonne's, beside her creative talent, that needs to be in this book is her cooking. She has fed our family for all our married life, whereas I'm not even sure where in the kitchen the cooker lives.

One summer's evening, we were outside enjoying a meal that included mashed potato (Yvonne- style; it's delicious), when her blood sugars dropped particularly low. Thomas and I knew tea needed to be consumed rapidly to help Yvonne and to avoid her having another meal ruined by having to have slurps of Lucozade. Thomas was pushing his Mum to eat her potato. It's the nature of the Beast, especially if you have been a Type 1 for so many years, that the human body tries to adjust. Yvonne can function perfectly normally on a blood glucose reading of 2.5, when really she should be incapable of anything. Yet at other times she will be struggling with a figure higher than that. Yvonne does get defensive if being pushed in these circumstances - no one can possibly understand including her family or any medical diabetic professional what its like for her at this stage but she describes it afterwards as she knows what she is doing and that it feels as if we are trying to hurt her. Anyway, after continued nagging by Thomas in particular, Yvonne picks up a lump of potato from her plate and launches it in my direction. It scored a direct hit (probably from her dart throwing days in the pub). I hadn't even said much! I did explain later that if I'd have wanted more potato I would have preferred it on my plate. We take this on the chin, or in our face and file it in the lighter humorous side of what she goes through.

Yvonne will say she didn't achieve much but going from a Personnel Officer to a Trust Board Executive, raising two kids whilst putting up with this unforgiving condition just in my time is remarkable by any standards.

As you've read, but it needs restating, she was also Prime Carer for her mum, my mum, whilst full-time working, and then my auntie Val, her dad and now her step mother. Her empathy for people suffering, together with her experience and knowledge of the NHS and its wider care community, makes the job she does as a carer incredible. Yvonne must take all the credit for her performance, tenacity and the effort she puts in to looking after people, even though she will try and give credit to others. That's why I and our kids and a couple of friends have staged a bit of a coup here and taken over this chapter. To show you the sides of Yvonne she is too positive and upbeat and even modest to talk about. She doesn't blow her own trumpet – or saxophone – so we've taken over the story to help you see what we see.

There, I've said my bit. I feel Harriet at my elbow wanting to take up her mum's story from her point of view. Over to you, darlin'."

Our adopted family member

"Diabetes has been a part of our family from as long as I can remember, like an adopted family member. But when I think of Mum there are so many other D-words that I think of first: Determined, defiant, daring, dedicated, delightful; diabetic is way down the list.

My first memory was doing show and tell at school on the importance of Mum's Lucozade. I was five. The small bottle of lucozade she carried with her at all times was ingrained into me early on. I'd like to think I gave my classmates a lesson in the condition.

We mustn't pretend the relationship with diabetes was always benign or easily managed. I remember occasions when she'd be shouting in the night, going into her bedroom and seeing Dad trying to lift her to give her Lucozade (the night hypos were always worse because she obviously wasn't aware of how low her bloods actually were when asleep). Seeing your mom limp or even rigid sometimes, shouting and not making sense was frightening and some nights I would hide under the covers and put my hands over my ears. As I got older, I would go in and help Dad, holding Mum's hand or pouring the Lucozade into her mouth.

Over the years you learn about ways to handle Mum's hypos and how to talk to her, or to the adopted family member, which is how I occasionally think of the diabetes, who is peeping through defensively. When the bloods go low, the person can realise they are at risk, that there is a threat to their health, and an autonomous defensiveness kicks in. The threat is externalised and the person has to defend themselves against it, with sometimes comic results. Mum often refuses Lucozade and will do anything to stop you giving it her, for example moving her head away. Anyway, she had once again gone low and Thomas was trying to give her Lucozade. He was getting nowhere, and they were both getting more and more agitated. I was trying not to get involved, as you don't want her – the defensiveness that kicks in - to feel 'attacked', which is how she describes the feeling during these moments. Sometimes you can see the fear in her eyes.

Thomas tried one more time to push the bottle to her lips and … she kicked him hard right in the shin! The look on his face as he dropped to the floor (classic football player move) compared to Mum who didn't bat an eyelid, was extremely funny! I took over as the one 'rescuing' Mum, and she took a drink. The adopted family member has turned us all into psychologists. Good cop, bad cop is a useful tactic in these situations, so the bad cop draws the fire of the defensive reaction. I hope Thomas isn't reading this as he'll have clicked what role I cast him in when these situations occasionally arise. Better go buy some shin pads. Or, better, we could adopt Mum's friend Gillian's brilliant tactic on the odd occasion a hypo signals it is on its way. When at a restaurant with Mum, Gillian noticed Mum had suddenly gone quiet, wasn't her usual chatty self, and was refusing her Lucozade. Her blood sugars were dipping and she needed to counter it. Quick as a flash, Gillian sticks a full wine glass of lucozade in Mum's hand, says "Drink up your Prosecco, Yvonne. Enjoy!" And down it went, including all the sugar in it that she needed in that moment. Sweet as a nut.

As you can tell, one of the best ways of defusing any dips the adopted family member may take us down is a sense of humour. Laughing at it disempowers the downside of diabetes and reframes how we see it, as something special and empowering. A superpower even, as one of mum's friends describes it. Mum's sense of fun is so strong that it conquers all, so to speak. For example, she hadn't long had her pump when we were out shopping at the Bullring. I can't remember exactly when it was but, sadly, another terror attack had been on the news and security were everywhere. It was very busy and as we were going down the escalator we were chatting about it.

I said, 'What would we do if someone exposed themselves as wearing a bomb now?' She replied without missing a beat, 'I'd go up to them, show them my wires and say I've got one too, as a distraction." Yes, it was a joke, but also a classic example of her tendency to jump in and help in an emergency; I wouldn't put it past her to do exactly what she was joking about. Trying to save the world, one person at a time, is part of Mum's makeup, one of the uncountable things that make us so proud of her and the adopted family member when it comes to defining who my mum is.

Although I said in the beginning there have been negatives to seeing Mum live with this lifelong condition, there are also many positives. The positives are entirely down to her and how she manages it. Yes, she has bad days, but these are rare. She throws herself into keeping busy being a mum, nanny, friend and head of the family. I cannot put into words how she has inspired me, particularly now I am a mum myself.

I cannot begin to imagine how she raised a family whilst working full time, particularly when she reached the high position in the NHS that she rose to. All whilst managing and controlling her diabetes. Not only that, but she has so many other strings to her bow: floral design, completing charity challenges (swimming the equivalent length of the channel – twenty-one miles or 1,352 lengths of a 25 metre pool). There aren't enough words. So, I will end on this: my mum is my best friend, my inspiration and I strive to have her strength. I hope I am making her as proud of me as I am of her.

Hold on Mum. Before you divert us with tales of partying, someone else wants a word. This is a 3D story of your life and who you are, and that needs this outside-in perspective to give the rounded version and balance out you downplaying your achievements and not realising, perhaps (so the reader needs to be told by us) how central your life is to the lives of so many others. I'm handing the keyboard over to a couple of your dearest friends for their side of your story. The hijack continues …"

Wendy and Gill's Yvonne

"So, dear reader, as Yvonne likes to call you, you've read about her from husband and daughter. Here's the friends' experience of Yvonne. Our names are Wendy and Gill. We first became friendly after chatting on the touchline as we cheered on our kids at football over twenty years ago. (Our children are the same age.) Yvonne soon became integral to my (Wendy's) family and was a pillar of support during a few very difficult years, helping emotionally and also practically, with the children, when needed. Most importantly, we all had fun together, enjoying many New Year's eves and Christmas evenings (I nearly destroyed the Xmas tree at one; she forgave me). Yvonne threw legendary parties, open to oldies and children alike, which is part of the *joie de vivre* she brings to her own life and those lucky enough to be part of it.

Our children shared many milestones together. Yvonne had to put up with Tony spending endless hours organising and coaching all our sons football team. Yvonne and Tony helped set up my new home in 2001, even driving down to London to fetch bunk beds, erecting them on the same evening after the long drive, arranging my flowerpots and cushions (Yvonne has an eye for design).

When my husband died in 2002, Yvonne was there. She pampered me after a gruelling bereavement counselling weekend and got to know my parents and siblings well. They all lived in London but were reassured to know that Yvonne was keeping her eye on me up in the Midlands. Life continued with all its fun, trials and tribulations and our families remain close. Yvonne was there for me when my daughter was very poorly following a hospital stay in 2010, even driving over in the middle of the night when I was extremely worried. And looking after my elder daughter for a few days while I stayed in the hospital.

In 2011, Yvonne and our close friend, Gill, arranged a fabulous surprise party for my 50th birthday, creating an amazing event. I was thoroughly spoiled and extremely touched. Designing incredibly creative parties, especially surprises that create joy and lifetime memories for other people, is just one of Yvonne's many passions that she pours her heart into.

Right, this is Gill taking over the story. During those birthday preparations came my first encounter with Yvonne's diabetes. When I first knew Yvonne, I learnt she was a Type 1, had a pump, frequently pricked her finger and always carried a very large handbag! It was a while before I realised what diabetes actually involved for Yvonne, and that length of time says it all; it definitely doesn't define her. The diabetes doesn't say 'NO' to what she does in life. it is in fact the opposite, a spur, a 'you watch me' motivation that encourages her to live life to the full. That's what she means when she refers to it as her best friend (not including us, of course). So, for example, we were out organising Wendy's birthday celebrations, as described above. On the way back, we stopped off at a local pub for some well-earned refreshments. We were deciding on a snack when I noticed Yvonne had stopped her usual chatting. She'd gone quiet and seemed quite agitated. At first I thought I had offended her, but then the penny dropped. I knew she drank Lucozade when her sugars were low, so my next challenge was to get the Lucozade from her bag. I tried asking nicely, finally gave way to expletives, grabbed her bag, thinking, "This could be the end of a beautiful friendship", and held my breath. Mission accomplished. In went the Lucozade.

It didn't ruin our relationship; she is lovely inside and out, finds humour wherever she can and diabetes has to work around her life, not the other way round.

Right, this is the Wendy half of the friends' double act back again. We celebrated Yvonne's birthday in the Lake District that same year. A very large group of people who all valued their respective friendships with Yvonne and Tony gathered together. There was much fun and many adventures. To say Yvonne is the life and soul is an understatement.

Her ability to lift you in good times and bad is legendary. Yvonne was there to comfort me when my mum died in 2018 and my dad in 2020. And she celebrated with me when I remarried in 2021, not only attending the church and reception, but arranging, preparing and delivering the bouquets, table flowers and buttonholes for the big day itself, ably assisted, of course, by Gill.

Most importantly, Yvonne has done all this despite her own challenges with diabetes, which are not insignificant. Rather than using this as an excuse not to do things, I believe it drives her forward. She is extremely positive, fun loving, caring, creative and an inspiration. Of course, Yvonne is human, and has her own 'moments' but she always comes up smiling.

Another friend is tapping on our shoulders, wanting to share her Yvonne with you. Over to you, Anne."

Gill, moi, Wendy

Anne's Yvonne

"She hasn't told you about the running, our Yvonne, has she. In June 2005, I completed a beginners' running course with Dudley Ladies' Running Club. My husband, knowing that I wouldn't continue running on my own, suggested I run with the wife of one of his running mates. And so the adventure of being part of Yvonne's life, that still continues today, began for me.

Yvonne and I (with two other friends, Pauline and Gill) no longer run, but we have had many adventures in the years between then and now, with many more to come. We always plan ahead - have Lucozade and Jelly Babies ready, phone and blood machine on standby just in case, and have on occasion needed all of them. There have been times in the middle of a run when there has been a call to Tony to pick us up because legs and eyes have suddenly become particularly wobbly. On one urgent occasion there was a "Come NOW Thomas please" and Thomas did indeed drop everything and come running.

Yvonne has supported me and I her. I have dragged her over the finishing line (literally) at the British 10k race in London and managed to avoid being pushed in the cut and told where to go on a beach in Biarritz. But these last events weren't Yvonne. That was her little constant companion, Diabetes.

Few people have the privilege of walking alongside (or running alongside) and gaining just a little insight into the constant pressure experienced by someone with Type 1 and the skill and constancy with which they manage it. It's not quite being in their shoes but you become a close witness and participant. I am always in awe of how Yvonne never lets it get in the way of our exercise, social time and our trips out, of how she keeps diabetes in its place as just an aspect of who she is. She respects it and looks after it but doesn't let it dominate. She shows how to embrace diabetes and still live life to the full (and more) so that we who love her have grown to understand and embrace it, too. I have to echo what Gill wrote above: Yvonne is lovely inside and out, finds humour wherever she can, and diabetes has to work around her life, not the other way round.

OK, Yvonne. You can have your story back. Write on."

Sunday Girls' capital effort

THREE Stourbridge mums pounded the streets of London in the British 10K to help raise charity cash to support Special Olympic athletes close to their hearts.

Anne Cruchley from Pedmore, Yvonne Warner from Hagley and Pauline Evans from Stourton – nicknamed the Sunday Girls after the day of the week on which they train – were among 25,000 runners who took part in the event on Sunday July 6.

Pauline's daughter Rebecca also took part in the run, which the team completed in aid of Special Olympics Great Britain.

Half of the £2,000 they raised will go to the national charity while the rest will go to the Worcestershire branch, based at Bromsgrove's Ryland Centre, where Stourbridge Special Olympians Amelia Martin and Alicia Bradshaw train.

Yvonne said: "We took on on the challenge with the aim of raising as much sponsorship and money as we could for this very special cause which helps to deliver year round sports training and competition for people with learning disabilities."

Melinda Martin, mum of Clent Special Olympian Amelia, said she was "grateful beyond words" to the

● **Anne Cruchley, Yvonne Warner, Pauline Evans and daughter Rebecca.**

team for their support of the branch, which has made her daughter a sporting star.

Amelia, who competes in the 100 and 200 metre sprints and the 200m relay, represented Great Britain in Prague in 2005, Rome in 2006 and took part in the World Games in Shangai in 2007.

She also won three gold medals in Spain in 2008.

Alicia gained gold medals for the 200 metres and 100-metre relay in

London in April and she hopes to be selected to run in Los Angeles next year.

The Sunday Girls, who staged a series of events ahead of the race to help rake in funds, have completed a couple of charity runs in the past and following the success of their latest outing they plan to organise one each year.

To boost the team's fundraising total visit website www.justgiving.com/thesundaygirls.

211

Thomas's Story

"Hold on. Thomas here with a tale that reveals a side of Mum - her daredevil side - that I think is missing from this book. Each year, we head off on an annual family/work trip to Northern Ireland to see John, Julie and their family. The 2017 trip turned out to be a break of a different sort for Mum. The wrong kind.

Picture the scene. Everyone else, including me, is cosy in bed. Mum, Dad and Julie step out for an early morning hike in the rain. The weather sets in. It's dark, it's wet and getting wetter. They cut their losses and take a shortcut home through a field. But there's an obstacle, a brook that needs to be jumped over.

Dad gallantly offers Mum his hand. Mum, typically, refuses it and makes the jump. There's a loud crack and a gasp from Dad and Julie. Mum thinks she's just twisted her ankle. Which wouldn't account for it being stuck out at a right angle. Having refused her hero's gallant hand, she then has to accept Dad carrying her (thank goodness for his Iron Man capabilities) for a quarter of a mile across the fields.

Julie calls ahead to Johnnie, who jumps into his car to get as close as possible. I, in a panic, have to phone home to Sis, who is in even more of a panic until I explain the details, as she knows Johnnie's propensity for mountainous walks. Johnnie gets close, guided by a woman who, whilst broke off walking her dog, ran to the meeting point while the dog stayed alongside my mum. Mum's bundled into the car and rushed to Coleraine Hospital where, amid a shower of apologies, her clothes are cut off to reveal ... a number of significant fractures and a complicated dislocation. It was splintered. Dad is still in shock to this day from watching four doctors pull the foot back into position from its 90-degree broken angle, without full anaesthetic.

Mum had to be flown back to Queen Elizabeth Hospital, Birmingham, to be operated on. But you're not allowed to fly if you're anaesthetised (hence the four docs tugging without anaesthetic).

After ten days of amazing care - ankle rebuilt, scaffold-like, with plates, screws and bolts, similar to that of Big Ben recently - she returned to her own building site (the house was being renovated), which included climbing a ladder to bed, held and pulled by Dad and I. One night, navigating her way through the dim hallway (temporary builders' lights) on crutches, she went a over a girder that was lying across the hall. Dad and I came running to find her in fits of laughter on the hall floor in the gloom. But it wasn't just the invalid who went flying. I forgot the girder too and, on my way back from the kitchen with a plateful of food, did my own spectacular somersault, plastering the walls with sandwiches.

Some adventures you want to go through again. Others not so much. Though we look back and laugh (Mum does anyway), the broken ankle escapade is not one we'd like repeated, thank you Mother, as I'm sure you wouldn't. Right, having revealed her daredevil side to you, I'll hand back to Mum."

Take time to party

Charming. My party stories get squeezed into a corner of this chapter by the sudden appearance of a band of fellow authors, my fabulous life partners in crime. Well, I love them for it. Life isn't something you live on your own (hopefully so for you, dear reader) so it's only right that those you love who live it with you help to write it.

My life so far, as a person diagnosed from childhood with Type 1 Diabetes, has been overwhelmingly happy. I mean the joy in my life far outweighs the downsides. In fact, my forever best friend adds urgency to the need to seize the day, to make incredible memories, ensure life is full of adventures. That's what makes it a superpower. It adds an intensity to the need to celebrate life. In my family that means parties. I only have space here to describe a few.

Throughout the years, Tony and I loved to throw a good party for family and friends. The pleasure you get from everyone having a good time is awesome. The day after, when surveying the clearing up, you say "Never again!" Until it's time to organise the next one.

I told you about Tonys 30th Birthday party, back in the day. Well, key milestone birthdays became a bit of a thing, especially milestones marking a decade lived for each of us. For each of our 40th, 50th, 60th birthdays, it became a mission to outdo each other in the surprises.

For Tonys 40th, I hired a band and a marquee for our garden although, given the enormous size of the marquee, it more or less took over the garden, which gave up and disappeared under it. The band had been runner up on New Faces (for those of you who remember that far back). Just to give you an idea of the impact: My sister-in-law Jackie's mum Joan was on the way to the party with Jayne, Jackie's older sister. As they got to the traffic Island a quarter of a mile away, Joan said, "Listen to that racket!" Jayne said, "Mother, that is where we are headed!"

Jackie, later that evening, raided my knicker drawer and threw them on the stage when the band were singing Sex Bomb, the Tom Jones classic. Mum would have loved it. She would have been crying into her handkerchief. Thank God my knickers were clean and sexy in those days. The youngsters, my little nephews and Harriet, had a great time purloining the coke bottles, shaking them up until a fountain of coke erupted.

The challenge was on for Tony, not to be outdone, for when my 40th came around. He hired the Lodge in Wellington Road Dudley (Lenny Henry would know it). I'd been told I was just going out for a meal, so it was a shock when I turned up. I should have got the hint earlier, when my friend Deb picked me up at the house, took one look at me, said, "You're wearing that?" and took me upstairs to upgrade my outfit for the night.

Instead of the swanky restaurant at The Belfry I thought we were headed for, we arrived at The Lodge, where I was mystified to see Dad in the car park directing cars. I walked in and Harriet, and all her tiny school friends, aged 8-9, ran over to greet me. The place was overflowing with my family and friends. What I didn't know was that Tony and Deb had secreted my saxophone in the boot and I was hauled up on stage later in the night to play it. Thank goodness the band drowned me out. We have the video to prove it. We also have footage of Harriet's friend's mum, me and my 80 year old deaf Black country Auntie Edith on stage performing Long Tall Sally. What a night. Our neighbour's husband, who couldn't be there as he was a policeman on duty, made a cameo appearance, popping in with his uniform all ripped and roughed up, having chased and caught some thugs earlier in the evening.

Follow that. Ten years later we did, when it was my turn to surprise Tony on his 50th. I hired a local village hall. At the time I was doing my floral design course, so of course my friend and I did all the table decorations, along with photos of Tony's 50 years. The entertainment was sublime. To open, we had Tony's best friend's daughter Robyn (who was teaching Harriet the flute) and Harriet playing The Flower Duet from Delibes. Tony loves his classical music. He had a lump in his throat when his running mate, stood next to him, said "They are miming that well", and Tony's chest puffed up so much as he whispered back, "They are not miming mate." The surprises continued: his best mate Paul sang a Bruce Springsteen number (we'd been to see the real Boss at the Villa a few years previously). Then it was all rounded off by our son (aged 12) making his first speech and toasting Tony. How many more tears and proud moments could you get in one night? But it didn't finish there. His running club mates (I've still not forgiven them) had bought his entry to do his first Ironman (26.2 mile marathon, 2.4 mile swim and 112 mile bike ride, a total of a 140.6 miles). I dragged Tony to our solicitors the following week and drew up our wills. He hasn't looked back and has competed throughout Europe. We're so proud of our Iron Man. He has provided us, his family, with so many other wonderful experiences, shared with our family and friends whilst raising a lot of money for charity. I also took him to Reid's palace in Madeira to celebrate his 50th, with Harriet and Thomas, for a superb meal. Not sure the kids appreciated it as much; maybe they can take Tony and I there sometime in our dotage, for our 100th.

Tony pulled the rabbit out the hat the year after for my 50th birthday. We were in the car, the four of us, going to stay for my birthday weekend with my brother, Jackie and nephews Richard and Michael. Tony had booked us a room at a lovely hotel nearby. Or so I thought. We get to Graham and Jackie's, and the neighbours are there, and champagne is popped, and Jackie proceeded to usher us out to the local hotel, where we were having a meal, me with the most beautiful flower balloon in my arms. We get to the hotel and I'm ushered into the restaurant to be greeted by all my family and friends from back home. I'm still in shock today. We had a lovely meal and then I was kidnapped (with my permission). I was blindfolded and bundled in the car. We drove for what seemed an eternity, arriving in the back of beyond in the Lake District, at a Bunk Barn, where the partying began and lasted all weekend.

Next day, after a girls' day out at the spa, we jostled for the showers to get ready for the evening. I was in for more surprises: my college flower mate had done the flowers for the table, and everyone had turned the Barn into a beautiful venue. Jackie came to get me, as I was not allowed anywhere near until all creations had been completed. My bloods were not good, so I held back. Jackie was getting anxious, and a lot of whispering was going on between her and the men. The tension was rising. I think it was the first time Tony may have wanted to resort to drink. Twenty minutes later I was fit to go with repaired make-up (when your bloods go high the make-up disintegrates with all the perspiration). I walked into the Hall to find even more of our friends had come. The earlier whispering from the men suddenly became clear when the music started and my Brother, as compere, announced, "Ladies and gentlemen, for one night only …" On stage trouped my husband and family friends, dressed to undress for the finale scene from The Full Monty. No-one knew; they had kept it a surprise from their families, practising at Tony's mate Paul's, at the tennis club and even at Sainsbury's one time, when Keith bumped into Tony one night and they started practising the steps in the aisles. The resulting performance was fabulous, brilliantly choreographed by Keith. The evidence is still up on You Tube today. The next day was more celebrating: my cake, with Superwoman on it, was unveiled and cut. The icing on the cake, literally, was that it said "30" instead of "50". I was made up. My friends didn't sue the cakemaker but gave her a bonus instead. All of us, very much the worse for wear, then completed a treasure hunt throughout the Lakes, including a trip on the Windermere ferry, which became very competitive. Thank you, my Big Bro, for organising a brilliant end to a fabulous Birthday weekend.

We have had many more themed parties, from Pokémon, to football to treasure hunts for the children. We have had themed New Year's Eve parties - in fact, New Year's Eve themed Balls, including even 'I'm a Celebrity' themed, featuring the alternative Ant and Dec (alias Keith and Billy). I was still sweeping up maggots from the challenges two days later. More recently, for my daughters 30th, Harry Potter came to town. I was going through a particularly bad time, blood glucose wise, but held it together (thanks Soph and Abby) prepping my character and the party was a hit. Every party is a challenge: the work, the impact on my blood glucose levels. But it is so worth it: the memories far outweigh the lows.

Why party?

There have been yet more party landmarks in this adventurous life to mark each decade passed. I want to pause a sec in the midst of all this celebration to give you a context, though, in case you feel it's coming across as a bit decadent or Instagrammy. Here's the context, in the form of a statistic:

"Using life insurance applicants between 1950 and 1971, those diagnosed with diabetes prior to age 15 years had an elevenfold increase in mortality compared to that expected based on nondiabetic applicants, with a calculated life expectancy of 32 years for those with type 1 diabetes." – National Institute of Health

Did you get the implications of that? Of course you did. A few people understood this at the time. But, not many. As I recounted back in Chapter 4, I was at a school reunion when an old classmate walked up to me and said, "I wasn't sure you'd live long enough for me to see you at this." Tactless in the extreme, but with some truth there according to the statistics. And she was a rarity for knowing that. Most people in my life haven't known it and it's not something I've let them know. Which is why this book is something of a 'reveal' as they say, of the hidden side of my life, that I've kept even from people I love, as I don't want to worry them or be anything other than normal with and to them. Do you see now why building wonderful creative experiences with ten-year party highlights every time another milestone is reached is so vital? Literally? It's about celebrating an ongoing life and creating joy.

Tony's 60th and mine were lower key but still extra special. We took Tony to the Isles of Scilly and I bought him a flying lesson, like you do for your other halves on a special birthday. But this time I really started something. He enjoyed it so much, he booked up for more lessons and is now (tada) an Iron Man who flies, right up there with Tony Stark. My amazing husband has his pilot's licence. We have made many more lovely friends and have spent a few lovely times flying away to other climes and look forward to many more.

For my 60th, Tony, Harriet and Thomas created another spectacular event, themed around a film score. You must get by now how much I love a good musical. Mama Mia was the extravaganza laid on for me. My family and friends dressed up and sang exerts, which was fantastic. On top of that, my nephew, whom I previously mentioned was a cameraman, was in Sri Lanka filming The Good Kharma Hospital. He asked one of its stars, knowing he was my all-time fave actor, Neil Morrissey, to wish me a Happy Birthday. It's all captured on film to be relived whenever required.

Well, what will we do for our 70th's. That's for the future. Right now, I've got to get my Man over his 100km (62 mile) finish line for the Brighton to London race in April he is preparing for, to raise some more money for Diabetes charities. Maybe our 70th's will be material for my next book. Hopefully I'll still be here, living life to the full with my forever friend and constant companion, but not doing anything less than having the best time possible, surrounded by everyone who has helped me achieve the things recounted here and whom I love with all my heart.

My Full 50th Monty

Paddleboarding on Windermere eek !

Harry Potter came to Town

Another Warner Family Party

FINAL THOUGHTS

I hope you have enjoyed reading this as much as I have writing it, that it has given you a tiny insight into what life is like as a Type 1 Diabetic, that you can survive and thrive to tell a tale, or even your life story, living a life full of love and adventure, aiming high and picking yourself up when the odd fall happens, a life of highs, lows (literally, hypo wise) and everything else in between.

So many advances are now being made daily on improving the management of Diabetes through technology and moving towards a cure or a way of living with it more easily, with the risk to life removed from the everyday. My heartfelt wish is to be there when that is achieved, and I know it will be one day.

Type 1 Diabetic's life in numbers

During the time of Covid, I was awarded the Nabarro Medal for living with diabetes for fifty years. It was lockdown time so I couldn't receive the award at a ceremony in person. Instead, I bought a gift for each of the amazing members of staff in my Diabetes and Endocrinology clinic and circulated the gifts and this note to them as a thank you:

A life in numbers

In my fifty years a diabetic I've carried out on myself:

<u>10,000</u> urine tests

<u>170,000</u> finger pricks

<u>70,000</u> injections

… to keep myself alive and well.

BUT I would never have got through this without my wonderful family, friends and … YOU.

Never forget how much you are appreciated and that your input to someone who has spent their life attending clinics - your smiles, help and support – made it possible.

I COULD NOT HAVE DONE IT WITHOUT YOU ALL.

In the meantime, I will continue to love, laugh, dance, create, contribute to the lives of others, party (!) and bask in being surrounded by my growing band of earthly angels - Tony, Harriet, Ally, grandson Otis, Thomas and his future family. I hope this book helps them realise how loved they are. And how grateful I feel and how proud of them I am. And the same for the rest of my family and friends.

What I wish for you, dear reader, whatever trials and tribulations you may face in life, whether you have Diabetes in the family or anything else that could be seen as life-limiting is this: it doesn't have to limit your capacity for joy and love and happiness. If you are learning to live with diabetes, like little Yvonne, back there in that children's ward all those years ago, I hope you take away one thing from my life story so far; that if you look after your forever best friend, listen to their needs and never turn your back on them, they will look after you.

Yvonne Warner

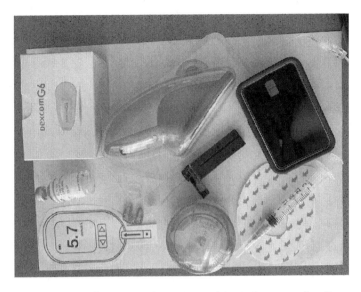

Just some of our everyday consumables to keep us alive & kicking

The family flying high

The Best

APPENDIX: 50 REASONS

During the Covid pandemic I lost my Dad, and received my Alan Nabarro medal for having lived with Diabetes for 50 years. My one regret is that Mum & Dad never lived to see that, because they were, with all of you instrumental in helping me achieve that.

Due to the Covid restrictions, I could not have a celebration or award ceremony but my family and friends ensured I knew just what party they would have given me. They also provided my daughter with their personal views on this key milestone achievement and she compiled this beautiful record for me.

I will treasure it forever.

50 REASONS YOU ARE AN INSPIRATION

1. You have lived 50 YEARS WITH TYPE 1 DIABETES!!!

2. You push yourself to live life as normal as possible.

3. You never give in to it. You stick to being healthy and in control.

4. You are always willing to 'give it a go!'

5. You were 9 years old when you had to start managing this chronic condition.

6. You try to see the positive in everything.

7. You stay up to date with the developing research around diabetes and educate yourself.

8. You are keen to learn about how to manage your condition and open to new ideas.

9. You raised a family who love you deeply.

10. You are determined and always think long term.

11. You always push US to achieve.

12. You juggled family life and managed a group of mental health hospitals.

WE CAN'T EVEN BEGIN TO IMAGINE WHAT IT IS LIKE TO LIVE WITH TYPE 1 DIABETES BUT WE WANT YOU TO SEE IT FROM OUR PERSPECTIVE BY **LIVING WITH YOU** WHO IS **LIVING WITH IT.**

13. You swam the length of the channel to raise money for those living with Diabetes.

14. You have weed in a pot 9125 times!

15. You have pricked your finger 165,000 times!

16. You have injected yourself 69,951 times...

17. You have drunk litres and litres of Lucozade and if we tell you it's a glass of wine you will drink it quicker!

18. You are always up for a challenge- Diabetes isn't a 'NO' for you.

19. You arrive extra early to airports to endure the 'strip search'.

20. You swipe yourself multiple times a day like an item going through checkout!

21. You choose not to be a professional thief even though you would leave no fingerprints.

22. You created a new purpose for bras... To support your pump as well as your boobs.

23. You calculate every carbohydrate that enters your mouth and you say you're bad at Maths!

24. You track every minute of exercise even as little as going for a walk which WE all take for granted.

25. You have never been able to carry a 'clutch bag'! Your handbag has to be big enough to carry ALL of your supplies!

26. You always put others first.

27. You make everyone feel at ease.

28. You are always willing to help someone by sharing your knowledge and experience.

29. You never judge anyone.

30. Your pain threshold is extremely high!

31. You smile on days you are finding tough.

32. You are so loyal.

33. You try to see the good in all people.

34. You find beauty in everything and make everything beautiful with your creativity.

35. You are beautiful inside and out!

36. You have a wicked sense of humour!

37. Diabetes never takes a break, (day or night) so you have to keep going too!

38. One of your vital organs failed you but you adapted and are responsible for your body to live.

39. You are a blood sugar detective... Investigating why your levels are not as expected or even questioning when they are right.

40. You are a model patient according to the many professionals you have encountered!

41. You are a 'go getter'!

42. You never make it an excuse!

43. Nothing phases you!

44. You can laugh about past hypos!

45. You tell great stories of your experiences.

46. You do not let it define you!

47. You are the strongest woman I know.

48. YOU HAVE GOT THIS!

49. You make Diabetes work for you!

50. YOU CONTROL IT AND IT DOESN'T CONTROL YOU

Printed in Great Britain
by Amazon